Rebels in the Front Yard

Liberty at Gettysburg

By David Cleutz

GETTYSBURG

PUBLISHING

Rebels in the Front Yard

Gettysburg Publishing LLC

Please go to www.gettysburgpublishing.com
for all our other titles

ISBN-978-0-9838631-0-6

Dedicated

To the memory of

Henry Alexander Clutz

Descendant of

Liberty Augusta Hollinger and Jacob Clutz,

and of Samuel Forney

*"The first casualty of the 75th Reunion of the Battle of Gettysburg,
July 1, 1938!"*

Foreword

Rebels in the Front Yard – Liberty at Gettysburg

Liberty Hollinger was a sixteen-year-old girl living in Gettysburg when the greatest battle ever fought on the North American continent erupted around her. With courage and strength, she dealt with the trials of occupation by the invading Confederate army. In her own front yard, she was witness to the fears of the South's greatest general, Robert E. Lee. For three days, she lived with the horror of battle. After the armies departed, she gave herself to the task of caring for the wounded they left behind. When time came for President Lincoln to consecrate Gettysburg's hallowed ground, she witnessed first-hand the President's deep sorrow. In her later years, at the Fiftieth Reunion of the Battle of Gettysburg, she witnessed the gathering of veterans Blue and Gray, when brotherly fellowship finally erased the bitterness of Civil War. Still, the traumatic events of the battle and its aftermath had left indelible memories. Near the end of her life, Liberty Hollinger preserved her memories for her family in a brief memoir. Its first-hand accounts are the basis for much of this book. While other authors have recently discovered the copy of her memoir in the Adams County Historical Society and included an incident or two in their books, this book contains all the material of her memoir, put in context of the events surrounding her accounts.

Before Liberty found rebels in her front yard, several other teens had their own harrowing encounters with the army that had invaded the peaceful Pennsylvania countryside. John Forney, 16, and his brother Samuel were plowing their father's field in Hanover, when they found themselves in the midst of a cavalry battle the day before the main armies collided in near-by Gettysburg. Their sister Susan, 18, tended the wounded of blue and gray in the Forney parlor. Next day their cousin, Maria Shultz, 19, found herself between North and South as they fought for control of Seminary Ridge in the first day of the Gettysburg battle. Her home became headquarters for three Confederate generals. These teens' eyewitness accounts have long been part of the author's family archives, and are also included in this book.

Countless books have been written about the Battle of Gettysburg, but few about the civilians in its midst. *Rebels in the Front Yard* provides the reader with a view of the experience not as seen by soldiers, but in the words of teenagers who lived there.

The sub-title, *Liberty at Gettysburg* has a dual meaning. Liberty is the name of the main character of the story. Liberty is also the prize America gained at Gettysburg. Abraham Lincoln in his Gettysburg Address spoke of the United States as "a new nation, conceived in Liberty". Victory at Gettysburg preserved the nation and indeed, led to true liberty for all.

Table of Contents

Prologue – Rebel Invasion!

It was mid-June, mid-1863, mid-Civil War. In the small towns and on the farms of the rolling southern Pennsylvania countryside, the citizens were roused from their summer routines by the unexpected arrival of the Confederate Army in their midst.

Up until now, war had been off in the distance – mostly down in Virginia, except for late last summer, September 1862, when battling armies had spilled across the Potomac into Maryland. The fighting at South Mountain and along Antietam Creek by Sharpsburg was close enough that some Pennsylvanians went down by buggy to view the results.

And then of course, there was that invasion of Pennsylvania by the swash-buckling Virginia cavalier, General J.E.B. Stuart just a few weeks later. On October 10, Stuart and 1800 cavalrymen crossed the Potomac River on a lightning raid up to Mercersburg and on to Chambersburg. The Rebel raiders took horses from the farms and helped themselves to whatever they liked in the town shops. They even tried to burn a bridge on the Cumberland Valley Railroad at Scotland – but found that ironwork doesn't burn very well. Next morning Stuart's band crossed over the South Mountain pass at Cashtown, and, passing up a visit to Gettysburg, turned south along the east slope of South Mountain into Maryland. With an embarrassed Union Cavalry in hot pursuit, Stuart escaped back over the Potomac to Virginia, virtually untouched.

Stuart's bold raid had caused quite an alarm along the way. But except for the unfortunate farmers and shop-keepers his men had visited, taking more than a few "souvenirs" of their trip "up North", Stuart's ride around McClellan's Army through the placid Pennsylvania countryside was soon out of mind. It was harvest time, and the hard-working families had to get the crops in, the apples picked, the apple butter made and the produce canned for the winter meals, the hams hung up to cure. The war seemed far removed from their daily lives.

But now, in the midst of another planting and harvesting season, war suddenly seemed a real threat. Lee's Virginians had crossed the narrow neck of Maryland by the Conocheague Creek. They had quickly moved across the Mason Dixon line. Now the Confederates, some seventy-thousand of them, were spread out and marching all across the Cumberland Valley, and beyond. Some were sent foraging west to Mercersburg at the foot of Tuscarora Mountain and then over the mountain to McConnellsburg, looting stores and farms as they went, before turning back to rejoin the main army at Chambersburg.

Others spread out across the broad Valley, moving all the way beyond Carlisle to the heights above the Susquehanna at Harrisburg. Some crossed over South Mountain onto the broad plain, passed north of Gettysburg, moved through York and headed toward Lancaster and Philadelphia, foraging in the prosperous Pennsylvania farmland. Lee's orders about foraging had been strict. They hadn't "raped and pillaged" – this was America, these men were Christians, after all, even if they were Rebels who hated Yankees. But they took what they needed. And these Virginia soldiers needed a lot. Barefoot, ragged, and hungry, the stores were cleaned out of shoes and clothing, the chicken-houses and smoke-houses (and it seemed like every householder had them, and often a pig, besides) stripped bare.

Very quickly, the citizenry responded to this threat to their peaceful lives. Some gathered up family and prized possessions and fled to the mountains, or north, where they hoped to be beyond Rebel reach. Not all were successful. Those that stayed, buried their valuables in the back yard and then did their best to fend off any marauding Rebel foragers.

All hoped that the invaders would pass through their neighborhood quickly, and move on to the cities that they assumed the Rebels were after – Harrisburg, Philadelphia, Baltimore (surely they weren't so bold as to try for New York!). None thought that their own Union Army would manage to catch the Rebel onslaught and give battle here, amid their fields, in their small towns. And indeed, the armies eventually moved on from Chambersburg, from Waynesboro, pulled back from Carlisle and York. As fate would have it, they would concentrate at a small village some eight miles east of South Mountain, eight miles north of the state border, south of Carlisle, north of Frederick Maryland. That village was called Gettysburg.

The Pennsylvania citizens weren't aware that just beyond the Mason Dixon Line, in Carroll County, in a thirty-mile long formation around Frederick, the Union Army had arrived, under its new commander, George Gordon Meade. Just to its east, the feared Virginia raider, J.E. B. Stuart, was moving north with his cavalry corps. Union cavalry commander Judson Kilpatrick was moving east from Littlestown. Both were trying to find the Rebel division of Jubal Early that had headed for York and Lancaster. As the days of June slipped off the calendar, Stuart and Kilpatrick were fated to collide at Hanover, 14 miles east of Gettysburg. At Gettysburg, ten roads converge, from all points of the compass. Confederate, or Union, forces were on each of these roads. A day after Stuart fought at Hanover, the main armies were destined to meet at Gettysburg. The citizens of Hanover and Gettysburg, like it or not, were about to welcome Rebels in the Front Yard.

Karle Forney owned a large farm on the southwest edge of Hanover. On June 28, 1863, his sons, John and Sam, went out to plow a cornfield across the road from the house. John, 16, never dreamed of what lay in store for him that morning – Rebels in the Front Yard.

In Gettysburg, the Forneys' teen-age cousin Maria Shultz went about her daily tasks, helping her sister and mother in the garden, cooking, sewing, putting up strawberry and cherry preserves for the winter. The recent incursions by Southern cavalrymen had caused some excitement in town. But in her comfortable house near the Lutheran Seminary on the west edge of town, Maria never dreamed that terrible fighting was about to surge up the Chambersburg Pike and surround their peaceful home.

On the other side of Gettysburg, Jacob Hollinger, wife Sarah Diehl, daughters Liberty Augusta ("Libbie"), Julia, Annie, Bertie and little son Augustus, ("Gussie"), said grace and had their usual Monday night supper. They lived in a solid, two-storey home on a large plot of ground between the York and Hanover roads, where they intersected at the east end of town. Like most small town dwellers of the 1860's, the Hollinger homestead had a barn and chicken coop. Their sustenance was built on their own resources.

Jacob owned a warehouse by the railroad, a convenient walking distance just two blocks northwest from their home. There he dealt in lumber and grain. As a young man, Jacob had moved to Gettysburg from the Hollinger family farm when he got a job working in the warehouse. By working hard and saving diligently, by 1863 he was the owner. He had met Sarah, a Chambersburg girl, in Gettysburg, likely when she was visiting her sister, Sallie Diehl, who lived there. His business had prospered. At 41, white-haired, he carried himself with a gravitas that made him a respected and valued man in the community. A devout man, he and his family were faithful attendants at Christ Lutheran Church, despite its being a number of blocks up York Street, past the Square on Chambersburg Street. It was the College Church. Pennsylvania College, soon to be re-named Gettysburg College, was a Lutheran School. The seminarians of the Lutheran Seminary also attended. So the quality of the homilies would have been far more thoughtful than a typical village church.

Now, on Monday, June 28, 1863, 16 year old Libbie Hollinger waited with her family, wondering what events the new week might bring. A Confederate presence had been felt in Gettysburg this past week – they had no idea that by Wednesday, they would be hosting Rebels in their front yard.

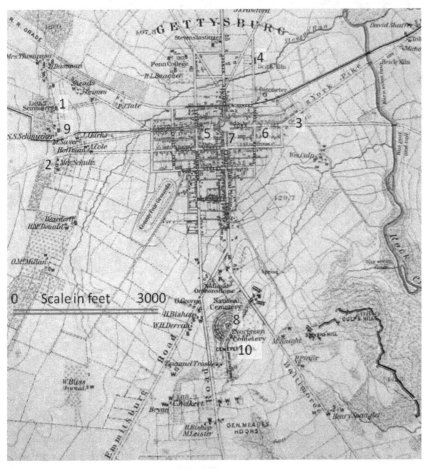

Map of the
Battle-Field of Gettysburg
Engineer Department, U.S. A. , 1869

Key:

1 – Lutheran Seminary	6 – Carpenter shop
2 - Maria Shultz home	(Confederate surgery)
3 - Liberty Hollinger home	7 - Wills house (Lincoln)
4 - Kuhn Brickyard	8 - Lincoln's Gettysburg Address
(Coster battle site)	9 - Rev. Dr. Jacob Clutz home, 1913
5 - Christ Lutheran Church	10 - Liberty & Jacob Clutz grave site

Chapter 1 Cavalry Battle at the Forney Farm

Karle Forney home, Hanover

Collection of Henry A. Clutz

Forney Manor

"Forney Manor", the Forney estate in Hanover had already witnessed much history. In the 1730's, this was the edge of civilization. An English king had declared this to be his land, though two of his subjects had then declared it theirs. William Penn's sons sold this piece of land to a Germanic immigrant, Adam Forney. He immediately set out to make it a farm like the one he'd left back in the old country. He soon found that he had to share the pure waters of the spring on the land with native American women and their babies. They may not have the parchment deed from the Penn brothers that Adam could show in court, but they had rights that came with centuries of use before the Europeans landed in Philadelphia and moved west. Adam wisely shared his water with the native Americans. He had more important fights.

The Carroll founders of Maryland also laid claim to this southern-most section of the land that the Penns were given by the king. Their sheriff came up from Baltimore and took Adam Forney off to stand trial for non-payment of their taxes. But his English was so poor that they sent him home and took another farmer south to be their test case in the courts. Ultimately, the fight was resolved by two English surveyors, Mason and Dixon. Their line settled the boundary between Pennsylvania and Maryland. A century later, that line would mark the division between free soil and slave states - a national division erased only by blood, in a great civil war.

Forney Manor had seen nothing but peaceful times since its construction in 1808. The war with the English known as The War of 1812 had indeed come close, with the movement of the government to York, just miles to the north east. While below the Mason-Dixon line to the south, their Maryland neighbors still held slaves, the Forney family complied with Pennsylvania law and had freed theirs. Now, in the summer of 1863, Karle Forney, his family, and his hired help provided the labor that a large farm required. They worked hard, sun up to sun down. They may have discussed politics and the terrible impact of the war that had come upon the land, but their main concerns up til now were the demands of their farm and their family. Today all that would change.

Tuesday morning, June 30, 1863, began much like every day. John Forney, 16, was up at dawn. His mother served her family a hearty breakfast of eggs, biscuits, ham and scrapple. When the men left to start the day's chores, Susan, 18, helped her mother "rid up the table" of the breakfast dishes, preparing for a day's work canning vegetables fresh from their garden. Mary Ann Forney was a hard-working farm wife. She had instilled in her sons and daughter her dedication to duty and family. As a young woman she had written this motto in her "friendship book":

I slept, and dreamed that life was beauty.

I woke, and found that life was duty.

The sun rose in a clear blue sky, as John and his brother Samuel walked out to the stable and hitched up their plow horses. It was promising to be a beautiful June day – just what every farmer hoped for. The boys walked the horses across the Littlestown road to the cornfield and hitched them up to the plow where they had left off at sundown the night before. They were about to witness one of the opening rounds of what would become the Battle of Gettysburg.

While the boys had been eating breakfast, two large troops of cavalry were saddling up and riding down the roads that led past the Forney farm on the southwest edge of the village of Hanover. Coming east on the Littlestown road was Brig. Gen. Judson Kilpatrick's division of Federal cavalry. Coming north on the Westminster road was Maj. Gen. Jeb Stuart's corps of Confederate cavalry. They would collide at the Forney farm – the Battle of Hanover would have the Forney family in its midst.

Forney boys watch the Yankee Cavalry

The boys had been following the plow up and down amid the rows of growing corn plants for nearly two hours when something attracted their attention. Looking back toward their house and barn, coming up the road from the direction of Littlestown, was an amazing sight - a dusty column of mounted men that seemed to go on as far as the eye could see.

This was something special. The Forneys had heard that soldiers had been seen in the area during the past week, but now here they were, in their midst. The plow-horses got a break, while Sam and John clambered up on the fence rails to watch the parade of men on horseback heading into Hanover. As they approached, John could see from their blue coats that these were Federal cavalrymen. The boys watched with great interest as the horses passed by them.

First came the dashing young general Judson Kilpatrick. His reputation for hard-riding and aggressive fighting had been hard on both horses and men, earning him the "behind his back" nick-name – "Kill-cavalry". His staff rode along beside, their horses prancing as they relished an upcoming break at the watering troughs in the village.

At 8:30, Kilpatrick's troopers having passed, the next column of Federal horsemen arrived with an equally flamboyant general, George Custer, his hair flowing, at the head of the line. Custer had only just been promoted to Brigadier, given command of a cavalry division in recognition of his devil-may-care aggressive cavalry charges. As the soldiers rode past, the Forney boys called out to them. An occasional cavalryman, likely just farm boys themselves not long ago, would halt and pass the time of day with the young farmers on the fence rail. Unaware of the impending battle, the good-natured banter was a welcomed change for both soldiers and Forney boys.

16

"A Soldier in gray coming yonder"

Looking down the road, the boys saw amidst the line of blue coats, a rider dressed in gray. Samuel Forney later remembered his interchange with a Federal Lieutenant. "You have a soldier in gray coming yonder."

"Yes, he is a scout. We captured him up the road. He is our prisoner now." The Confederate rode up to the boys and stopped his horse. "So you are plowing corn. I often plowed corn myself down in North Carolina, before I entered the army. I am a soldier now, but I wish I were back in my native State, working in the fields quietly like yourselves, for this is a cruel war and I hope it will soon be over."

The boys watched for a while longer, but duty called. They got back to work. The horses moved at a slow pace drawing the plow between the rows of corn. It was around ten o'clock when a third Federal column approached up the road from Littlestown, led by yet another dashing young new Brigadier, 27 year old Elon Farnsworth.

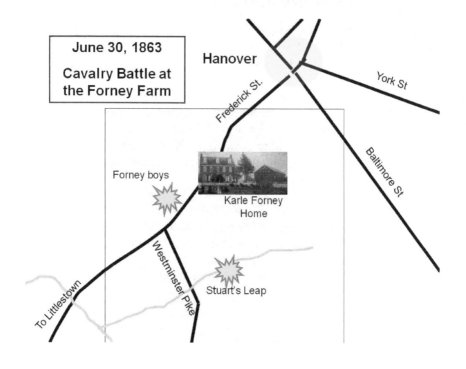

June 30, 1863

Cavalry Battle at
the Forney Farm

Hanover

Frederick St.

York St

Baltimore St

Forney boys

Karle Forney
Home

Westminster Pike

Stuart's Leap

To Littlestown

Boys in the crossfire

Farnsworth and his men passed by on the road between the cornfield and the Karle Forney house when Sam and John heard shouting and yelling, coming from just down the Westminster road. It was the 13th Virginia Cavalry, part of Jeb Stuart's Cavalry corps, galloping up to attack Farnsworth's rear guard, the 18th Pennsylvania Cavalry. Coming up the road, the Confederates were headed right toward the Forney brothers. The Virginians, whooping and hollering with their Rebel Yell, let loose a volley with their carbines at the Pennsylvanians.

Sam Forney: *"In a few minutes, the fields immediately north of the Littlestown road and west of Hanover were filled with mounted soldiers. The Union troops had immediately fallen back through the town to the assistance of the rear regiment that had been attacked."*

Confederate Cavalry Charge

Painting by Reuben Becker

Collection of The Guthrie Memorial Library, Hanover

with permission

The Battle of Hanover had begun, right there in Karle Forney's fields, and his boys were caught in the middle of it. Bullets were whizzing past, their horses were spooked, the young corn was being trampled. It was time for these two civilian farm boys to leave the field to the combatants, to head for cover!

Amid the shrieking and yelling, Sam, as the elder, gave the order that John was more than ready to hear. "Unhitch the horses, John. We must get out of this battle before the horses are shot. Father would never let us forget it!" John likely thought "And Mother would never forgive you if I was shot!" And so they untied the harness straps and with a "gee" and a "haw" hustled the two terrified animals across the field toward the McSherrystown Road, away from the bullets whistling around them. They found safety for both horses and men in the barn of their neighbor, Geiselman. After listening to the boys' long and fervent description of the battle next door, Geiselman insisted that they remain with him until late in the afternoon, when the battle had ended.

Back at the Forney house, there were indeed Rebels at the front yard. This was no peaceful visit. Karle and his wife and daughter looked out the windows at the road in front. Horses and riders were enmeshed in a grand melee, sabers slashing, pistols firing, carbines shooting. Farnsworth's Pennsylvania troopers were giving as good as they got. Pennsylvanians fought Virginians and North Carolinians with courage. This was their state - their ground. These Rebel invaders would learn that Yankee cavalry would not give it up easily.

When stray bullets hit the house, Karle hustled his family down into the cellar, remaining there as the battle ebbed and flowed into the streets of Hanover, then back out along the road in front. The Confederates had emplaced two artillery pieces by a lime kiln behind the Forney barn, and were firing at the Union forces north of the town. Huddled in the cellar, Susan Forney and her parents listened to the booms and felt the ground shake as the cannons fired. Was this just the beginning of the great battle between the invading Rebels and the Federal army pursuing them? And what fate had befallen John and Sam? The boys were out there somewhere – had they gotten away to safety? Surely the Rebel raiders wouldn't shoot unarmed farm boys, would they? Susan could only hope that this was just an unexpected fight of mounted horsemen, one that would soon be over.

"Jeb" Stuart's Escape

Later, General J. E. B. Stuart arrived on the scene, and with his aide Lt. Col. Blackford, was struggling to extricate his Confederate troopers from the confused fighting in the streets, to pull them back to the south of town. Blackford would later recall: "In spite of all we could do they got past us, and before we were aware of it, we found ourselves at the head of the enemy's charging column." They fled south down the Westminster road, lined with a high hedge on the side of the fields south of the Forney house and barn. Finding a gap, Stuart urged his horse "Virginia" to leap the hedge into the field, only to find that a Federal force of some twenty riders were there, flanking the main body. They shouted "Halt!" But Stuart and Blackford galloped on, the Federals following in hot pursuit, firing their pistols as they rode. The Virginia cavalier suddenly found himself in danger of being trapped. In his path was a deep, wide gully formed by a stream. He didn't slow - at the very edge, Stuart dug in his spurs. His thoroughbred horse Virginia, though tired from many long days' rides, sprang forward, carrying Stuart up and over the ravine onto safe ground.

Blackford tells the story of Stuart's escape: "The field was in tall timothy grass and we did not see, until close to it, a huge gully fifteen feet wide and as many deep stretched across our path.... I shall never forget the glimpse I then saw of this beautiful animal away up in mid-air over the chasm and Stuart's fine figure sitting erect and firm in the saddle. The moment our horses rose, our pursuers saw there was something there, and it was with difficulty they could pull up in time to avoid plunging headlong into it. General Stuart galloped on up towards the top of a hill to direct the fire of a battery on the pursuing regiment."

Jeb Stuart's Escape

Painting by Reuben Becker

Collection of The Guthrie Memorial Library, Hanover

with permission

Rallying his troopers, Stuart held them in readiness on the hills south of the town in an uneasy truce with Kilpatrick's men down in the village. At nightfall, under cover of darkness, Stuart and his cavalry slipped past the waiting Union troopers. He led his men east toward York, then on to Dover in the northeast part of York County, riding hard to rejoin General Ewell's Confederates in Carlisle.

Chapter 2 After the Battle of Hanover

Next morning, with things quieted down, the Forneys emerged from the cellar, only to view the scenes of destruction on the street and in the fields around the house. Wounded cavalrymen had earlier lain scattered on the side of the Littlestown Road. Many had already been taken away to temporary hospitals in Hanover. But several had made their way into the Forney front yard, and onto the front porch. When she saw these wounded men, Mary Ann, as a good Christian, immediately invited them into her home. With Susan's help, she managed to get the men into her parlor. Once there, she realized one of them was a Confederate – a Rebel. The fight between them was over. Here in the parlor, all these men were fighting a common enemy – Death. Knowing the Confederate lying next to them did not have long to live, the wounded Federal troopers asked Mary Ann and Susan to first see to his needs.

Twenty horses lay dead along the Westminster road between the Forney house and their neighbor to the south. John, his father and brothers spent most of the day helping to drag the carcasses away. When they got back to the house later that afternoon, they found their parlor had become a make-shift hospital. Three wounded Union soldiers and a Confederate trooper were being cared for by his wife and daughter. Mary Ann fed them broth and bread, while Susan did her best to tend to their wounds.

Susan comforts a wounded North Carolina trooper

Sergeant Samuel Reddick, 2nd North Carolina, had been wounded, shot in the chest and unhorsed, in the melee on the road in front of the Forney house. As the fight went on around him, he managed to move out of further harm, into the front yard. He dragged himself up the steps onto the front porch, where he lay for several hours, until the family discovered him with the other wounded men and took him inside.

Sam Reddick had seen hard fighting during the first two years of the war. His 2nd North Carolina Cavalry was the smallest regiment of "Fitz" Lee's Brigade of Jeb Stuart's Division. This was not his first visit to Pennsylvania. His regiment had been part of Stuart's raid into Mercersburg and Chambersburg back in the previous October. That highly successful ride around McClellan's Army, just a few weeks after Lee's defeat at Antietam, had helped restore the Southern morale. It was perhaps the inspiration for Lee to embark on the current invasion back into Pennsylvania, this time with his whole army.

But Stuart's raid this time was not doing Lee any favors. His route had been so far to the east that he was unaware of the Union army position, and too far from Lee to provide him the scouting reports he needed. Stuart's fight on June 30th at Hanover had accomplished little but to further delay his rejoining with Lee at Gettysburg until he was too late to be of much use. More than a few Southern newspapers would later blame Stuart and his ill-advised raid for the fate that would befall the Army of Northern Virginia at Gettysburg in the next three days.

Sam Reddick's October visit to Pennsylvania had been a happy one. Like all the Rebel troopers, he rode back to Virginia on a fresh horse, and probably, leading a spare, all courtesy of unwilling Franklin County farmers. He would have felt well fed, courtesy of those farmers' chicken coops, and well-stocked smoke houses. Today, his second visit had ended, abed in the Forney parlor. Though Mary Ann Forney was seeing to it that he was fed, and Sue was doing her best to make him comfortable, this visit was not going to end well, he knew.

Sam Reddick was struggling to stay alive. Susan, by her tenderness in caring for him, soon earned his trust. With much difficulty, he reached into his jacket pocket and took out a small book. It was a copy of the New Testament. Opening the cover, he showed Susan a name on the fly-leaf – that of his sister, living back in North Carolina. Susan bent down near to him. With the little breath he had left, he managed to make this last request.

Take this book, and send it to my home. That address will reach my sister. She gave me this book when I left home two years ago, and she asked me to keep it and bring it back again when the cruel war shall have ended. It has ended now for me.

Sue promised him that she would do as he asked. She stayed there in the parlor consoling him as he breathed his last. The wounded Union cavalrymen had already been transferred to a military hospital set up in the Pleasant Hill Hotel on Baltimore Street. Only the Forney family remained to mourn Reddick's death. Karle and his sons dug a grave for him under a group of locust trees along the fence by the road, where Reddick had first fallen to the Federal bullet. They gave him a Christian burial.

Sue Forney honors a Confederate's last request

As good as her word, Susan Forney wrote to Reddick's sister, returning the New Testament that had been carried through so many battles in the past two years. That began an exchange of letters with Reddick's family in

North Carolina. Reddick's father, a clergyman, wrote to ask that his son's grave be marked with a cross. Of course, the Forneys had already done so. In the meantime, the senior Reddick had heard from another North Carolina cavalryman who had been wounded and sent to the hospital in Hanover. He told Mr. Reddick that his son had been buried "near a red barn with a slate roof, within a hundred yards southwest of Hanover" – the Forney farm. A year later, relatives came to Hanover, took up the body of Sergeant Samuel Reddick, and returned it to his home town in North Carolina. There his body was re-interred with honors in the village cemetery.

Forney farmstead in later years

Samuel Forney farm at Hanover
Collection of Jennifer O. Herring

In the years after the war, John Forney moved west to set up shop in Steubenville, Ohio. Samuel, as the eldest son, inherited the Karle Forney farm, shown here little changed from the day of the battle. With him are his wife and three daughters – Laura, Minnie, and Elizabeth.

Chapter 3   Seminary Ridge – Rebels in the Parlor

Wednesday, July 1, the day after John and Sam Forney survived the cavalry fight at Hanover, their cousin Maria Shultz had her own encounter with the invading Confederate Army. Maria, 19, lived with her widowed mother Elizabeth and older sister Cornelia in a large brick home on Seminary Ridge at the west end of Gettysburg, just down the road from the Seminary. Elizabeth Forney Shultz, was Karle Forney's sister, Sam & John's aunt. She had married a successful Hanover lawyer, David Shultz, and had later relocated her family to Gettysburg. She and her daughters had moved away from what would become the site of the cavalry Battle of Hanover, but now found themselves in the midst of the greatest battle of North America, at Gettysburg. Living on Seminary Ridge, they would be right in the heart of the first day's fighting.

Early Wednesday morning, just up the road from the Shultz home, Union Cavalry General John Buford climbed up into the cupola of the Seminary. From that high vantage point he was able to show the freshly-arrived General John Reynolds the on-coming Confederate army, moving in from the west. They were observing Confederate Major General Henry Heth's probe toward Gettysburg. That had led to battle with Buford's dismounted cavalry, first at Herr's Ridge, then shifting east to McPherson's ridge. Reynolds hastened to meet his First Corps troops just arriving from up the Emmitsburg Road. While he was directing them to move into battle line, a Southern sharpshooter's bullet knocked Reynolds from his horse – dead.

Artillery from both sides were firing from 8 am to 11am, when Heth ordered his men to pull back, obeying Lee's order – "don't bring on a general engagement". Lee wanted to be sure all his troops had arrived near Gettysburg, first. All along, his plan had been to catch Meade's Union army with its units spread out, so as to destroy it piece-meal. He didn't want to find himself in a situation where Meade could turn the tables and catch Lee's army elements and attack them one by one. And so the fighting had largely ceased before noon, except for the occasional artillery exchange.

The fighting had been contained to the ridges west of town along the Chambersburg Pike. Still, the booming firing of the big guns had shaken the nerves of the citizens of Gettysburg. Word spread: "the Rebels are going to shell the town!" Folks in the west end felt the most concern, but nervous families all over town packed up hastily and left their homes to head south away from the conflict.

The Gettysburg Lutheran Seminary, 1863.

from the photograph

"Scenes from the Battle-Field at Gettysburg, PA - The Seminary"

by Frederick Gutekunst

*Courtesy of Special Collections/Musselman Library, Gettysburg College,
Gettysburg, PA.*

During a relatively quiet noon time, reinforcements arrived from both armies, drawn by sounds of the morning's conflict, and by couriers hastening to tell their commanders that advance elements had met and fought at the little town of Gettysburg. Richard Ewell's Confederates came down from Carlisle and re-ignited the battle with Union First Corps units on the hills and fields north of town. Union general Oliver Howard sent his Eleventh Corps through the town to counter the Confederate attack. Howard wisely held back some of his artillery and infantry to hold the high ground on which sat the town's Ever Green Cemetery. He recognized that this high hill at the south edge of the town would be a crucial defensive position if his troops had to fall back.

General Meade was still in Maryland. Although a Pennsylvanian, he had never been to Gettysburg. And his fellow Pennsylvanian John Reynolds was now dead on the battlefield. So he sent another trusted commander, Maj. Gen. Winfield Scott Hancock, to assess the situation. Hancock took control, agreeing with Howard that the town cemetery was an ideal fall-back position if the battle got out of hand.

Mid afternoon, General Lee arrived on the scene. He had wanted his Army of Virginia to avoid a general engagement here, at this time. But a battle was already underway. So he reluctantly ordered Pender's Division to reinforce Heth's attack on the Union troops west of the Seminary. What had begun as small fire was about to become a conflagration that threatened to consume the town.

By 4 o'clock, heavy fighting was raging along the Chambersburg Pike, south along McPherson's Ridge and north along Oak Ridge to the Mummasburg Road, then in a battle line east to the hill that would become known as Barlow's Knoll. It was named after the Union brigade commander who first defended it before being forced back by two Confederate brigades. His men were forced to run or be captured. Down Stratton Street they ran, not stopping until they reached Cemetery Hill, where Hancock was re-forming a defensive line.

Back to the west, Heth's Confederates were being driven back. Lee ordered William Dorsey Pender's division into the fray. Pender's fresh troops charging past Heth's retreating men, pushed the Federals out of their defensive line on McPherson's Ridge. Despite their commander's death, Reynolds' Federals had fought on bravely and tenaciously, holding the line at the Lutheran Seminary. But at 4 o'clock, a bloody thirty minute charge by Pender's North and South Carolinians forced Reynolds' men off Seminary Ridge. Their regiments badly depleted by the day's fighting, facing superior numbers of Southern troops, the Union soldiers had no choice. Moving in good order, Reynolds' men went through the streets of Gettysburg to join Hancock's new line on Cemetery Hill.

The Confederates held up as the day grew late, and made Seminary Ridge their main line of defense for the next two days. There they placed their cannons, ready to support the assault they expected to make the next day. General Lee set up his headquarters in a stone house on the Chambersburg Pike at Seminary Avenue. Down the avenue, closer to the Fairfield Road, two of Pender's commanders came up to a brick house, the home of the widow Shultz.

Brig. Gen. James Lane commanded Pender's Second Brigade, Brig. Gen. Edward Thomas the Third Brigade. Lane, 29, was a North Carolinian like Pender, also 29. Both were military graduates, Pender from West Point, Lane from Virginia Military Institute. Thomas, a Georgian, was 38, and a graduate of Emory University.

When Dorsey Pender is wounded during the next day's attack on Cemetery Hill, Lane will replace him. But before the third day's battle, Lee will give command of Pender's Division to Isaac Trimble. Trimble will be wounded leading the division during the attack on Cemetery Ridge now known as "Pickett's Charge". Trimble will be carried to a temporary hospital set up in the Lutheran Seminary, just a block away from the home of the widow Shultz. There, after the battle ends, Trimble will be visited by two young girls, Libbie and Julia Hollinger. But that would be in the future. On this Wednesday evening, generals Lane and Thomas were about to become unexpected guests of the Shultz household on Seminary Ridge.

Rebel generals knocking on the door

James Henry
Lane, CSA

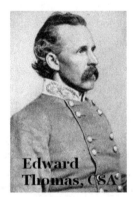

Edward
Thomas, CSA

William Dorsey
Pender, CSA

During the nerve-wracking afternoon amid fierce armed combat, the Shultz house had become a hospital. Elizabeth Shultz and her daughters Cornelia and Maria had taken in a number of wounded Federal soldiers, being treated by Union surgeons. Now, as the fighting came to an end, the Union troops who had fought by Shultz house were replaced by victorious Confederates. While Elizabeth and Cornelia assisted the surgeons treating Federal wounded men in the front of the house, Maria answered an insistent knocking at the back door. Reluctantly, Maria was forced to open the home to several high-ranking Confederate officers and their staffs. Confronting her were Brig. Gen. James Lane, commanding a brigade of North Carolina regiments, and Brig. Gen. Edward Thomas, commanding a brigade of Georgians. They were soon joined by their division commander, Major General William Dorsey Pender. Though gracious and considerate, these were the enemy. These were not "Rebels in the front yard", but "Confederates in the parlor".

The Shultz women were staunch Union supporters. Elizabeth's son David was a Major in the 73rd Pennsylvania Volunteers. He had enlisted in 1861, and fought in all the major battles in the East as part of Howard's Corps. Today his corps arrived in Gettysburg, but without him. David was in a Washington hospital, recuperating from a wound during the Battle of Chancellorsville while fighting Lane's Brigade, the same troops that now surrounded the house of his mother. Now here she was, forced to entertain the very enemy officers responsible for her son's wounds.

Elizabeth Shultz had no way of knowing it, but General James Lane had been responsible for an even more disastrous wound at Chancellorsville. It was North Carolina soldiers from Lane's brigade that had fired into Stonewall Jackson's scouting party, mortally wounding the General. Robert E. Lee said of Jackson's death, "I have lost my good right arm." Many historians have since attributed the Confederate defeat at Gettysburg to the absence of the formidable Jackson. So ironically, it could be argued that Elizabeth Shultz, in hosting General Lane, was repaying the man responsible for Lee's defeat at Gettysburg.

Maria Shultz later described her experiences during the Battle of Gettysburg, when she had Confederates in the Parlor.

We expected only a skirmish between raiders when the opening crash began, but were carried along with the excitement and laughed to see the civilians and non-combatants fly before the retreating and hard-pressed soldiers, until all the fences went down

31

and the cavalry drew up around the house, in the yard. Bullets crashed into the front and back windows, and the dead, dying, and wounded lay all around us.

A few minutes later, Generals Lane and Thomas stood at the door, speaking to me, when General Pender and Captain Adams, of his staff, rode up. General Thomas explained to them that there were three ladies, entirely alone, living in the house (Mother, my sister, and I). While I was talking to the Southern officers at the back door, Mother, (who was seventy years old) and Cornelia were in the front of the house with the surgeons and Union wounded who learned that the Southern army held possession.

Maria complimented on her courage

Amid the confusion, the day passed, finding us in the middle of the victorious [Confederate] *army, with every man ready to help us and attend to the few wounded left behind in the hurried flight. After dark, I was called on to take the lamp and go down in the cellar with adjutant Whitaker of North Carolina* [Lane's Brigade], *to hunt for concealed prisoners, but found none. We passed through the next three days in the midst of the Confederates there, receiving the most considerate attention from all, including the generals. All of us were highly complimented on our courage.*

Seminary Ridge became the Confederate line for the remainder of Lee's army's stay at Gettysburg. Pender's Division was in line around the Shultz home, with Longstreet's entire corps extending the line well to the south. The Union line mirrored it, along Cemetery Ridge to the east, south of the town. The long line of emplaced artillery aimed at the Union line must have given great pause to Maria and her family. Surely they were aware that across the valley an equal number of Union big guns were aimed at Seminary Ridge. One can only imagine the fear and worry the women felt, huddled together in the cellar during the massive two hour artillery barrage on Friday afternoon preceding Pickett's Charge. The ground shook along Seminary Ridge as the Confederate cannon fired round after round, and as Federal cannon balls struck the earth along Seminary Ridge in response. Elizabeth, Cornelia, and Maria, standing fast in their home through it all, had earned every compliment on their courage!

Chapter 4 July 1: Morning on Stratton Street

Early Wednesday morning, the first day of July in the year 1863, Jacob Hollinger walked up York Street, headed for his warehouse around the corner of Stratton Street by the railroad, a block east of the Gettysburg train station.

Rain showers during the night had left the ground damp, the air heavy. It was not yet uncomfortable, but Jacob knew that as the sun rose higher, the day would turn hot, and probably muggy, as it often did this time of year in Gettysburg. He had no way of knowing just how hot it was about to be, that afternoon at the warehouse, and hotter still in Kuhn's brickyard just beyond it. The "heat" there would be far deadlier than the oppressive humidity of a typical Gettysburg summer afternoon. And in the coming days of July, Jacob Hollinger and his fellow citizens would experience consequences of heat the likes of which they had never felt, and would never want to endure again.

Now 43, Jacob Hollinger had remained at home when the Civil War began, when younger men of Gettysburg had gone off to fight. With long white hair and a flowing white beard, he looked "much older and quite venerable", his daughter Liberty recalled.

He passed by the brick and clapboard homes tightly bunched together as is typical of Pennsylvania towns in the 1800's. This was a walk he had taken every day for many years, from home to work. But today, the first day of July in 1863, had the air of something different. He had a feeling that today was about to mark the end of his normal routine. He knew there were dangerous forces moving in the area. Confederate soldiers had already passed through the town, headed east. They had made little impact. Perhaps that was the pattern he could expect. Yesterday Federal Cavalry had also passed through town, looking for the Confederate invaders of Pennsylvania. The potential for serious mischief was certainly increasing.

No matter, he had to get to his warehouse and handle the day's affairs. Hollinger and his wife Sarah had moved from the family farm near Heidlersburg to Gettysburg some years before, when Jacob found work at the warehouse. After years of hard work and careful saving, he now owned the grain and produce business. If rebel forces should arrive in Gettysburg, he was going to do his best to protect his hard-won investment.

Grim-faced neighbors bade him a quick good morning, then hurried on about their business. One or two stopped and wanted to share rumors of soldiers and horsemen in and around the town. Were they ours or theirs, they wanted to know. They wanted to get the businessman's respected opinion. Was the town in danger? Was he leaving town for safer territory? Should they? Jacob offered no advice, other than he was staying. He had a business to run, and a warehouse full of goods that needed safe keeping. The rest was in God's hands. Let others worry. Jacob Hollinger had no special knowledge, despite the flood of information that his customers had given him the day before.

Union Cavalry was in the area, spread out in an arc around the west and north of the town. Confederate and Union cavalry had been in a big fight at the Forney farm on the edge of Hanover, just 14 miles down the road from the Hollinger house. Word had come in late in the day on Tuesday that Kilpatrick's troopers had driven off the dreaded Confederate raider, General J.E. B. Stuart, who had headed north toward Carlisle. A farmer from Arendtsville, on the edge of South Mountain northwest of town reported that a large body of Rebels had been seen at the Cashtown Gap.

As word got around, some citizens packed their belongings and made a hasty departure, convinced that war indeed had come to their peaceful town. Others, of a mind with Jacob Hollinger, were determined to stay. Some were confident that the Union cavalry would protect them. Others, less sanguine, were more concerned that a horde of Rebels would soon infest the village, looting any unguarded shops or houses. They would take the risk and stay, to try to fend off such southern vandals.

They had reason to be concerned. Friday last, June 26, a troop of Virginia cavalrymen rode into town up the Chambersburg Pike, whooping and hollering, firing their guns in the air, intending to use "shock and awe" to intimidate the townspeople. The raiders proceeded to ransack stores, barns, and chicken coops. Riding on up York Street, past the Hollinger home, and on to the crossing at Rock Creek, the Virginia troopers ran into a contingent of the 26th Pennsylvania Emergency Infantry. These men, college students, farmers, householders from the Harrisburg area, had been in service but four days. It was no contest. The Pennsylvanians scattered. One of them escaped capture, rode back into town and south on the Baltimore Pike, where other Virginians caught up with him and shot him. George Sandoe was the first Union soldier to die at Gettysburg, five days before the main battle began. Fortunately, in their haste to deal with the Pennsylvania fighters, the cavalrymen spared the Hollinger household any pillaging.

Any further depredations were stopped by General John B. Gordon, whose Georgia infantry regiments marched into town behind the Virginia troopers. General Jubal Early, whose division was encamped north at Mummasburg, rode into town and demanded that the borough provide food and supplies, or else $5,000. His demand was refused (the small town didn't have that kind of money). Early settled for the contents of a rail car that had brought supplies for the Pennsylvania Emergency soldiers. When Gordon's men spent the night in Gettysburg, the citizens had to endure the strains of Confederate martial music played by the brigade band. Jacob Hollinger had remained at his warehouse, keeping it locked. Gordon's men were content to empty the rail car near his warehouse, but leave that building undisturbed.

The next morning, Saturday, June 27, Gordon's soldiers marched out of town on York Street, past the Hollinger home, and over Rock Creek, headed for York. The Hollingers watched them go, relieved, hoping they had seen the last of the Confederate army in their town. They would later learn from friends near East Berlin (site of the Hollinger ancestral farm) that the remainder of Early's Division had marched through the area on the way to York to meet up with Gordon.

Sunday morning, townspeople on the way to church gathered on street corners and discussed the previous day's Confederate incursion. Someone said Union scouts had come into town and reported that the main body of the Union Army was nearby, a welcome sign that perhaps any further Confederate invasions would be forestalled. The Confederates had moved east, so if a battle were imminent, it would likely be toward York or Hanover. At Christ Lutheran Church on Chambersburg Street the Hollinger family joined the congregation in prayer, thanking God for sparing the town serious damage. Later in the day, a squad of Union cavalry rode into town, searching out the location of the Confederates. Having learned that Early's men had passed north and through the town, headed east, the troopers headed back south to report that intelligence.

Monday was quiet in Gettysburg. Perhaps indeed the danger had passed. That like many a summer thunderstorm, this feared storm of battle had passed to the north and east. But one local man wanted to find out if the Federal army was indeed headed toward Gettysburg from the south. He saddled up and rode to Emmitsburg. Encountering the lead troops of John Reynolds First Corps, he rode swiftly back to town to spread the news – thousands of Federal troops were just over the line in Maryland. The word quickly spread from house to house. Surely that meant protection for the town.

Unbeknownst to the Hollingers, movements were already underway that would bring thousands of Confederate invaders toward their town. Movements that when detected by the Federals chasing them, would put thousands of Union troops in motion to intercept the invaders. And all the roads converged at Gettysburg. If the Hollingers did have a good night's sleep on Monday, Tuesday would soon show signs of a coming storm.

Gen. George Gordon Meade, command of the Union Army of the Potomac thrust on him just days earlier, sent trusted cavalry units north from his Maryland camps to find out where the enemy was, and in what strength. Kilpatrick and Custer had ridden into Littlestown, ten miles east of Gettysburg, late Monday night. John Buford had crossed over South Mountain in Maryland and ridden north to Waynesboro, 22 miles west. Tuesday these Union horse soldiers would find the Confederate columns roaming through the ripe Pennsylvania farmland. Soon ominous sounds of battle would echo from nearby hills, the sound foretelling the storm to come as surely as distant thunder and lightning on a sunny summer afternoon.

"Great commotion in the morning"

Liberty Hollinger would later recall: *There was great commotion on the morning of Wednesday, July 1st, when the report spread from door to door that the enemy was coming in force. We could also hear an occasional boom of cannon west of town.*

She was hearing the artillery exchanges. First between Heth's Confederates and Buford's horse artillery, and then the booming increased as Reynolds' First Corps artillery arrived and began firing.

"Gussie" goes to town, as Rebels approach

Little Jacob Augustus Hollinger, just turned 3, had for the first time put on big boy pants. No longer would he wear a little child's dress. Swelling with pride, he begged his mother to allow him to go to the warehouse and show his father. His sister Libbie felt confident enough to agree to walk with the little boy up York to Stratton and on to the warehouse. *My brother Gussie, then a little lad of about three years, was eager to go to see father because he wanted to show him his first waist and breeches. I decided to go with him to please him, and also to hear what father thought about the situation. He did not seem in the least excited, and advised a little calm waiting for further developments. When*

I got home and turned into our gate I knew that the excitement was increasing. Many of our neighbors left their homes only to encounter greater danger elsewhere. Meanwhile, their houses were ransacked by the Confederates who took possession of most of the houses they found deserted and helped themselves to whatever they wanted, especially food.

Before noon, the people of Gettysburg knew that war had arrived on their doorstep – in the fields north and west of the village. The continual boom of cannon fire, the smell of gunpowder in the air, sent an unmistakable message. The conflict they had dreaded was indeed upon them.

Jacob Hollinger debated whether to lock up the warehouse and head home, or stay and try to protect his business. The word he was getting from excited men told him the fighting was still going on west of town, so his family and home were for the moment safe. He trusted his elder daughter, Libbie, to remain calm. She could reassure the younger children and her mother, who tended to be a worrier, that the family would be all right until he could get home at the end of the day.

Chapter 5 July 1: Taneytown Road

A farm boy along the road to Gettysburg

Jacob Clutz, at 15 just a year younger than his future bride Liberty Hollinger, had grown up on the family farm a few miles south of Gettysburg on the Maryland border. The 200 acre farm was nestled in a bend of Rock Creek in the southwestern-most corner of Mt. Joy Township. It had been purchased by his grandfather Henry Clutz in 1790, a parcel in a large tract that was known as "The Manor of Maske". Jacob was the youngest of nine children. On the sultry July morning, he took a noon-time meal break, perhaps in the shade of a tree by the Taneytown Road. He would have seen the dust of the marching columns of blue-coated soldiers, marching north at a quick pace. He would have then seen the men of the 134th New York, part of Col. Charles Coster's Brigade. Of course, he had no way of foreseeing that two of its officers would soon be saving his future wife and her mother from the battle's harm.

The boom of cannon fire was heard by the Clutz household that day and during the next two as well. But the fighting never got closer than about five miles away to the north. Jacob was too young to enlist, or to be involved in the fighting. He stuck to his chores on the farm until the fall, when he enrolled in the Gettysburg Academy.

Jacob had been infected with the spirit of patriotism that came over on the town during the first anniversary of the great battle of Gettysburg. When school ended on July 5, 1864, at age 16, he enlisted and served in Warren's Rangers, Mounted Infantry, officially the Pennsylvania Volunteer Cavalry. His discharge paper describes him as 5 feet 5 inches tall, blue-eyed, with light hair. He completed his service and was discharged on November 30, 1864.

Unlike the Jacob Hollinger family, the Henry Clutz family was little impacted by the Battle of Gettysburg. But Liberty Hollinger and Jacob Clutz would find themselves sharing the experience of the Battle in later years.

Chapter 6 July 1: A fiery afternoon

Arriving 11ᵗʰ Corps gives hope the town would be safe

By mid-afternoon, the situation was becoming grim. The sounds of cannon fire and musket rattling were coming closer, now to the north as well as west. Hollinger didn't know the details, only that heavy fighting was going on out along the Harrisburg road, and from the sound of it, was headed his way. He hadn't seen the movement of Reynolds' Federal troops moving up from Emmitsburg to Seminary Ridge, or Howard's bluecoats moving up Washington Street to the fields along the Mummasburg Road. He had no knowledge of which Confederate armies had arrived to contest the fields with Reynolds and Howard. The approach of A.P. Hill's Confederate Corps from Cashtown, or Ewell's Corps from Carlisle and York took place beyond his notice. He had no idea that Reynolds had been killed, or that Howard was in charge of the Union army at Gettysburg. He only saw the results. And felt the concern for his warehouse. Would the Union troops fend off the attacking Southerners? Provide a measure of protection for his business and his family?

Defeated 11ᵗʰ Corps men pass the Hollinger home

In the fields to his north, between the Carlisle and Harrisburg roads, Howard's Eleventh Corps was arranged around Blocher's Knoll, but would soon be outnumbered and out-gunned by Ewell and Rodes' Confederate Divisions. Gordon's Brigade, who had marched through Gettysburg on the way to York the Saturday before, was back, poised to drive the bluecoats off their knoll. At the warehouse the thunder of cannon grew louder. The guns were getting closer to town. Hollinger watched as disorganized groups of Eleventh Corps soldiers rushed by on Stratton Street, heading for safety on the hills south of town. Some passed by the Hollinger home, where Liberty and her family were on the porch, deeply concerned by the sight of retreating Union soldiers. Liberty later recalled:

On the afternoon of the first day's fight, when our men were falling back, a very young Union soldier came into our yard, and asked mother to keep his blanket and knapsack for him. He said he was not well and that they were too heavy for him to carry. He told her that if he never got back for them she should keep them. We never heard from him again.

Then they saw, coming up Stratton from the south, a column of Union soldiers moving at the double-quick, headed for the scene of battle. It was half-past three. After they passed his warehouse, Jacob Hollinger realized that some soldiers had stopped and gone into position near the train station just a block west, others coming down the track toward his warehouse. From them, he learned that this was the 73rd Pennsylvania regiment. He knew a Gettysburg man, David Shultz, had enlisted in the 73rd, and wondered if he was among the men at the station. He also learned that the 73rd was part of Charles Coster's brigade, that the men who had gone past were going to take up position just to the north, facing the open wheat fields from which the Confederates would be coming. These men told Hollinger that the soldiers were from three regiments – the 27th Pennsylvania, the 154th New York, and the 134th New York. Just 900 men trying to stem the Southern onslaught.

Coster's troops had marched swiftly from Maryland toward Gettysburg that morning. Around noon, his columns crossed the state line, marching past farms surrounding Rock Creek as it curled across the Taneytown Road. But they likely gave no notice to young Jacob Clutz watching them from his father's field as they hurried past.

Desperate fight near the Hollingers

After passing by the Clutz farm, Coster's Brigade hustled on to Gettysburg. They rushed on up Stratton Street and took up position on the north side of Kuhn's Brick Yard. Fighting valiantly along Kuhn's fence line, Coster's three regiments held out for as long as they could against superior numbers. They were but three Federal regiments, under attack by seven Confederate - three North Carolina regiments of Avery's Brigade and five Louisiana regiments of Hayes' Brigade. Soon taking fire from three sides, Coster's men had no choice but to give way. Those that could, ran back through the fields toward town, the Southerners doing their best to shoot them down as they ran. It had been a brief but bloody battle. A third of Coster's fighters were killed or wounded, a third captured. They had exacted a price from the Rebels – more than two hundred killed or wounded. But the Confederates now would control the town.

Among the Union wounded was Sgt. Amos Humiston of the 154th NY. As he worked his way up Stratton Street, past Hollinger's warehouse, he was shot again. Dragging himself into the back yard of a house on York Street, he lay down exhausted from loss of blood. Alone and untended, he took one last look at the Ambrotype that he had carried with him - the image of his children back in western New York, some 300 miles distant. The family of the house, inside, doors bolted, had no idea this young father had died near their back door.

Jacob Hollinger, seeing that the men of the 73rd Pennsylvania had abandoned their post at the station and headed south, remained inside the warehouse with the door locked. The North Carolina soldiers were chasing Coster's retreating men, firing as they came. The same Confederate bullets that had taken down Sgt. Humiston could just as easily maim or kill a civilian foolish enough to remain exposed to the line of fire. Hollinger would have to wait until the issue was more settled before quickly heading home to see to his family. He could only trust God had spared them harm.

The 134th New York, on the right of Coster's line, was flanked, and had broken first. Two young officers of the 134th, though wounded, were still able to run. Otis Guffin, 20, had been promoted to Captain of Company F just a month earlier. William Mickle, 23, had been promoted to First Lieutenant of Company E just three months before. Escaping the blistering musket fire, they ran due south through the brick yard and across the wheat field to the York Pike at the edge of town, headed for Cemetery Hill. Their line of retreat led right across the intersection of the York and Hanover Roads, past the Hollinger front yard. To the Hollingers, Otis Guffin and William Mickle would be saviors.

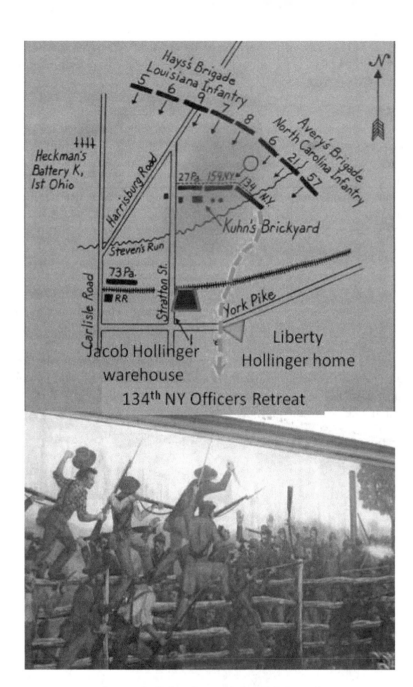

Coster's Brigade at Kuhn Brickyard

By Mark H. Dunkelman, with permission

42

Hollingers' New York "white knights"

On their front porch, Libbie Hollinger and her family listened fearfully to the thunderous roar of battle just a few blocks away. What fate was to befall them? The Confederate army was obviously in control of the battlefield, and approaching the town itself. Artillery shells were passing overhead. Cannons that General Howard had placed on Cemetery Hill were firing away at Ewell's Southern gunners firing from north of the York Pike. It seemed as if the Hollingers were in the midst of the cross-fire. Were both armies intent on shelling the town? Sarah Hollinger, overcome with worry and fear for her children and her home, had fainted dead away.

Responsibility for the family now fell to Liberty, the eldest of the children. What in the world was she going to do? How was she to keep the younger children and her mother safe from the destruction that seemed to be rushing toward them? Then help arrived. From New York's 134th regiment came her "white knights" clothed in blue, if not in shining armor. Two very brave men, wounded though they were, put aside their own danger to help a young woman and the younger children huddled around her.

Liberty saw Captain Guffin and Lieutenant Mickle approaching and sought their advice. She recalled: *While we were deliberating what would be best to do, two wounded Union officers came up, one a captain with a bullet in his neck, and the other a lieutenant with a bullet in his wrist. Both were suffering greatly. We appealed to them for advice, and they immediately asked about the cellar. They heartily agreed that it would be a safe place during the battle. We found mother lying in a faint from the excitement, and the officers first carried a rocking-chair to the cellar, then mother herself. They then said that they must hurry off or they would be taken prisoners by "Johnny Reb."*

In a little while General Howard's troops of the Eleventh Corps retreated through the town to Cemetery Hill past our house. They were closely followed by the Confederate troops and as we saw the gray uniforms, we thought with fear of the two kind officers who had delayed their departure in order to give us help and advice. We were very happy to hear from them after the battle that they had reached the Union lines safely, and later that they had recovered from their wounds.

As the two lines of soldiers ran past, firing as they went, we watched them through the cellar windows. Oh! What horror filled our breasts as we gazed upon their bayonets glistening in the sun, and heard the deafening roar of musketry! Mother was roused to consciousness by the terrific explosions and murmured over and over, "Have they shot at the town?"

Soon we heard that General Reynolds had fallen in the grove west of the seminary, now known as "Reynolds Woods." We felt then that we were indeed in the midst of a serious strife. General Howard's men had sought the hills south of the town, both for greater safety and to prepare for further battle in a stronger position.

Gettysburg spared destruction

Fortunately for Pennsylvania, the Confederates of General Robert E. Lee were forced to honor his Virginia gentleman's ingrained sense of what was fair in war. Civilians, as long as they behaved themselves, were to be treated gently. But had the Union army elected to hole up in the town, to make it a "safe haven", Lee would have given, albeit regretfully, orders to his cannoneers to shell the town. Fortunately for the residents, the Union commanders had chosen the hills around the town's Evergreen Cemetery as their haven, not the town itself. And so while Mrs. Hollinger might endure the indignity of rebels in her front yard, her family would be spared the deadly impact of cannon balls thudding into the brick walls of her house while she and her family huddled terrified in the cellar.

By the late afternoon, the day's battle decided, Jacob Hollinger locked his warehouse and walked home, unmolested by the Confederate soldiers who now were everywhere on the streets of the town. These men were exultant at their victory, but tired, and sobered by the losses they had suffered at the hands of these Yankees. Ground had been won only at great cost, and now the Federals were arrayed across the hills south of the town. A Stonewall Jackson might have inspired them, have pushed them to continue, to overrun the Federals in the hills before they could get dug in. But Jackson was gone, a casualty of the victory at Chancellorsville. And they were tired. Tomorrow would be another day. And after all, the enemy were Yankees. They always ran when really pressed. Tomorrow the Confederates would rise up out of the town and drive the Abolitionists from their hills, all the way back to Washington. Tomorrow, the South would win. Tomorrow, the Confederacy would gain its independence from these arrogant Northerners – or so they thought.

Arriving home, Jacob found his family safely in the cellar, unharmed, if yet fearful, and greatly relieved that he was back with them. He and

Libbie went upstairs intending to forestall any Rebel depredations on their family, while his wife and the younger children remained safe in the cellar. The Confederates that had chased Coster's New Yorkers out of Kuhn's brickyard into the town and beyond, were savoring the fruits of victory. They were helping themselves to whatever they could find in abandoned houses, and demanding what they wanted from the citizens that remained in their homes. Liberty and her family were not immune, but through the force of personality they were able to minimize the impact on their household. Liberty describes her family's confrontations with the Rebels:

Rebels savage the Hollinger Warehouse

Some of them rode into our yard and demanded the keys to the warehouse from father, who had locked it and come home when our men retreated. He refused to give them up, and they said calmly that of course they would get in. "Well," said father, "if you do I cannot prevent it, but I am not inviting you by giving you my keys."

Of course the Confederates forced the locks of the warehouse and took what they wanted and then ruined everything else. They opened the spigots of the molasses barrels and allowed the molasses to run over the floor. They scattered the salt and sugar on the floor also, and anything else that was accessible.

They then requested father to allow them to come into the house, and asked whether we would not cook and bake for them. Father again said "No," and when they insisted, Julia came to the rescue. When she stepped out of the cellar and said that it would be impossible for us to do so, it was as though a vision had appeared. Without another word they quickly rode out of the yard. She was at that time between fourteen and fifteen years old, a very attractive child, with dark brown eyes and beautiful brown curls, who always seemed to attract and impress strangers.

The same men came a number of times and wanted to take our horse and cow. Father always told them that the horse was too old to be of any use to them, and for the time being they left both the horse and the cow. There was a flourishing patch of corn back of the house near the barn. This was a temptation for their horses, but father simply told them that they could not use it, and wonderful to tell they never did. I do not know why they maintained such a gentlemanly demeanor unless it was father's silvery head

45

that awakened their respect. He was not yet forty-three years old, but his hair and beard had turned gray early and were as white as snow, making him look quite venerable.

Saucy Julia defies the Rebs

Julia was a spunky girl. No rebel was going to intimidate her. She was not about to give in to these invaders' presumptuous demands. It seems the invaders were gentlemanly enough to take the refusal by a pretty young lady with good humor.

The Confederates filled the town. They were appearing everywhere on the streets and taking possession of our neighbors' houses that had been abandoned. After making biscuits in a house across the street several called to Julia, who was on our balcony, and asked for butter for their biscuits. She saucily answered, "If you are hungry you can eat them as they are." They laughed and went back into the house.

Chapter 7 July 1, Evening: Liberty & Lee

Rebels in the Front Yard – Lee and staff

That evening, General Robert E. Lee rode east with his staff to consult with his Second Corps commander, Richard Ewell. While pleased with the outcome of the day's fighting, Lee was more intent on figuring out his next moves. This was not ground he had chosen for the battle with the Federal army. His troops were stretched from Seminary Ridge on the west side of the town, through the town itself, and around to the east across the York Pike and down to the Hanover Road. His enemy was concentrated on the high hills centered on the town cemetery. If he stayed and fought the next day, he would have to attack them there. Was it possible to hit them this evening, before they had a chance to reinforce their position? Were his troops ready to renew the attack after an already hard day's fight? Lee wanted to see for himself the hills to the southeast. These hills would, if in his hands, command the Federal right flank. And from that high ground, Ewell could roll up the entire Union line from right to left.

When Lee reached the east edge of town, he had an unobstructed view of Cemetery Hill, and to its east, the prominent high wooded knob that rose up past the fields behind the Culp farmhouse. Reaching the intersection of the York and Hanover roads, he reined in Traveler at the garden gate of a two story brick house. Taking out his field glasses, he inspected closely the terrain to the south as best he could in the twilight, then turned in the saddle and spoke to his staff.

Lee on his "splendid horse, Traveler"

Watching from the Hollinger porch, Liberty and her sister Julia walked to their gate, where they could hear the Confederate commander perfectly. Liberty describes the scene:

General Lee and his staff appeared in front of our house on the evening of the first day of the battle. I very well remember his face and striking appearance as he sat on his splendid warhorse, "Traveler." They were in front of our house for some time, while General Lee was observing, through his field glasses, the hills south of the town on which General Howard had taken refuge, and where now the whole Army of the Potomac was taking its stand to give further battle to the Army of Northern Virginia. After a long and careful examination he took his glasses down and I heard him say to the officers near him something like this: **"Those hills all around are natural fortresses. Wonderful! Wonderful! It will be very difficult to capture them or dislodge the troops holding them."**

Julia flirts with a handsome young Rebel in her front yard

Lee now realized that gaining the valuable high ground that was Culp's Hill would be a formidable challenge. But if he and his staff needed any further persuasion to forego the attempt, young Julia Hollinger was about to provide it. The pretty young teen was duly impressed by a young officer that sat on his horse by the fence. She took the opportunity to strike up a conversation, and perhaps flirt a bit with him, while still making it very clear where her loyalties lay. Liberty remembered: *There was a handsome young officer on General Lee's staff who backed his horse up quite close to the gate where Julia and I were standing. He presented a very striking figure, mounted on a beautiful sorrel with a red sash passed over his right shoulder and fastened at his waist in a knot from which the fringe fell over his knee. I think his name was Breckenridge. He seemed to give no heed to what his commander was saying about the wonderful hills on which our men were entrenched. Julia was telling the young officer how our troops were coming to Gettysburg from all points, and that soon there would be a formidable army gathered which they could not withstand. He looked at her quizzically and seemed amused, but he made no unkind or harsh reply. How much he believed we could not tell.*

Back at his headquarters on Carlisle Street, Richard Ewell awaited his commander's arrival. He was prepared to argue against any further attempts against Yankee positions on the hills on the south edge of town. His men were exhausted from hard marching and harder fighting that hot July day. Beside which, it was nearly dark. And dangerous risk awaited those who attempted night battles. His predecessor in command of Second Corps was the prime case in point – Stonewall Jackson, shot by his own troops who mistook his party for Yankee cavalry at Chancellorsville, returning to his lines at dusk after a scouting mission. No, Ewell, thought, he must convince Lee to wait for daylight to finish off this day's success. After his inspection of the Culp's Hill terrain from the Hollinger house, Lee realized that he would indeed have to wait for morning to renew the battle.

Hollingers tell Lee they will "soon be wiped out"

Lee was in the moment, focused on the important decisions of what would be the most momentous battle of the Civil War. He had no time or inclination for the kind of concerns his men might be feeling over the chances their Confederacy had of winning the war, even should they win this battle. Libbie had seen the concern in the eyes of the Rebels in the front yard: *Father kept telling the Confederates on every opportunity that they would soon be wiped out, as our men were coming in great numbers from all directions. What seemed to dishearten them more than anything else was that there seemed to be so large a number of able-bodied men left on the farms and in the towns for service in any emergency. All their men, young and old, were in the ranks, with no reserves left. They realized that the North could continue the war indefinitely, while they had about exhausted their resources.*

While Lee was considering the difficulties his men might face in taking Culp's Hill from an entrenched Federal force, Meade was moving his remaining army corps to Gettysburg. To the south, in Taneytown, Maryland, Second Corps had started the hard march toward the field of battle, some 13 miles north. The corps commander, Major General Winfield Scott Hancock, had left them at noon, sent by General Meade to hustle to Gettysburg to take command until Meade himself could get there.

Chapter 8   July 2:   The battle rages

During the night of July 1 and into the early morning hours, men on both sides rested as best they could. The wounded were in every available public building in Gettysburg. Confederate surgeons worked through the night amputating mangled limbs. The citizens that had remained in their homes slept fitfully, uncertain of what fresh disasters awaited when dawn would permit the fighting to begin afresh.

Hannah was as "brave as a lion"

Reinforcements that had arrived late in the day on Wednesday, moved into position on Cemetery Ridge alongside the survivors of that day's battle. The nine thousand troops of Slocum's Twelfth Corps had split up. Williams' division went east from the Baltimore Pike into bivouac southeast of Culp's Hill. John Geary's White Star Division went west, to "sleep on their arms" in a wheat field at the base of Little Round Top, the south end of Cemetery Ridge. There one enterprising young soldier found a local family to be very hospitable. James Hyde, bugler for Captain David Ireland of the 137th New York, wrote to his family: *As all was quiet, myself and a friend went to a house and stayed all night. We got some bread and milk, had a very good supper. Our brigade might move out at any moment but there was a very pretty girl there and we concluded to run the risk. The old folks were nearly scared to death, but Hannah was brave as a lion (before the fight ended, this house was very much shattered by the shells).* Young Hannah and her family would not be as fortunate as Libbie Hollinger and her family.

In the morning, James Hyde moved with his regiment and division to the east slope of Culp's Hill, anticipating the attack that Lee had ordered Ewell to make on Thursday. But Lee had given an ambiguous order that allowed Ewell discretion as to when conditions were favorable for the assault on the hill that Liberty Hollinger had heard Lee call "difficult to capture, or dislodge the troops". The Federals of Slocum's Twelfth Corps used the time to erect a long line of breastworks. Replacing them on Cemetery Ridge was General Dan Sickles' Third Corps. Sickles, ignoring his orders to extend the Federal Line south to Little Round Top, instead moved his line west. His resultant exposed position led to a near-disaster at the hands of General Longstreet's Confederates. His Third Corps was taking terrible losses at Devils' Den, The Wheatfield, the Peach Orchard. Late in the afternoon, most of Slocum's Twelfth Corps was ordered west from Culp's Hill to rescue Sickles. Slocum's remaining troops, a lone brigade under

George Greene, were thus left open to attack. Ewell now knew his attack could succeed. He sent three brigades to charge up the hill against the lone brigade of New Yorkers defending it. Fortunately for the Federal army, Greene's Brigade held off the Confederate attack Thursday night, holding the upper hill alone until nearly midnight when the rest of Slocum's troops returned to the hill.

Sharpshooters target Jacob

"Sharpshooter" by Winslow Homer – *Harper's Weekly*

From the end of the first day of the battle, the survivors from the First Corps had been manning the Union line along the north slope of Culp's Hill, facing the east end of Gettysburg. Their pickets were out in front, alert for signs of the Confederates preparing for a morning assault. When the sun rose, sharp-eyed riflemen in their ranks took aim and fired at any Confederate in the town that became visible in the early morning light. Any citizen up and about that Thursday morning had better be very careful to avoid being caught in the line of fire. This was a very real danger. Most citizens stayed in the cellar during the day, never venturing upstairs, let alone go outside.

Arising Thursday morning after a restless night's sleep upstairs, Sarah Hollinger made a hot breakfast in the dark kitchen and fed her family.

Jacob then sent his wife, Libbie, Julia, and the other children back down to the cellar, fearful of the battle that they were sure must come when the sun rose. Confident that his family was in a safe place, Jacob Hollinger then left the house. He wanted to see how his warehouse was faring at the hands of the town's occupiers. But first he had to milk the cow and feed the chickens. Normally, Libbie and her sisters would take care of them. But with fighting imminent, Jacob insisted that they remain in the safety of the cellar. As a non-combatant civilian, he trusted that neither army would deliberately try to do him harm. So he walked out behind the house to tend to his animals before heading off to the warehouse. Liberty described the danger he was walking into:

There was a large wheat-field south of our house on the Culp farm, ripe and ready for harvest, and it seemed to be full of Union sharpshooters. We could see them pop up and fire when any of the Confederates, especially officers, rode by. We could see them in the trees beyond also. When father left the cellar to feed the chickens or to milk the cow, the bullets flew all about him. Finally, he spoke to the sharpshooters about it. An officer said, "Why, man, take off that gray suit; they think you are a 'Johnny Reb.'" He put on a black suit and had no further trouble.

Jacob Hollinger had been fortunate to escape unharmed. The reality of the danger to Gettysburg's people living in the midst of the battle was brought home the next morning. Seeking a safer place to wait out the fighting, Jenny Wade, 20, had moved in with her sister, whose house was on Baltimore Street just north of the Cemetery. Despite the fact that Confederate sharpshooters had been firing at the upper windows of the house, presumably thinking Federal sharpshooters were hiding behind the curtains (they weren't), Jenny went up to the kitchen to make dough for the day's baking of bread. She wanted to feed Union troops as she had done on Thursday. A Confederate fired his musket at the door of the house. The minie ball pierced the door and hit Jenny Wade in the back, killing her instantly. She would be the only mortal casualty suffered by Gettysburg's civilians.

Wounded Rebels in the Front Yard

Thursday morning was ominously quiet, except for the occasional sound of musket fire from skirmishers to the south. Then in the afternoon, the Hollingers began to hear distant booming barrages of cannon fire beyond of the town off to the southwest. General Dan Sickles' Federal Third Corps was in a desperate fight with Longstreet's Confederate First Corps. Bloody battles were taking place on what had been peaceful farmland the day before – places that history would later remember as The Wheatfield and The Peach Orchard. Bucolic names that would forever carry a bloody memory. Others would carry a more sinister name – Devil's Den, The Valley of Death.

Meanwhile, wounded men from Wednesday's battle were still dragging themselves off the battlefield north of York Street, and hale soldiers were carrying in those wounded they found unable to move. Many of these, from both armies, stopped briefly at the intersection with the Hanover Road, perhaps heading for the improvised hospital that St. James Lutheran Church had become. Libbie Hollinger came out of the cellar only to find wounded soldiers, some Federal, some Rebels in her front yard:

The second day of the battle many wounded were carried through our yard on stretchers. Sometimes blood was dripping through the stretchers, and their faces were pale as death. Once in a while a man was entirely covered, too badly wounded to be seen. Some were able to help themselves and came limping through with the blood oozing from their wounds. One very youthful soldier in a blue uniform hobbled into the yard with a wound in his foot. The blood was soaking his shoe, and mother urged him to go to a hospital and have his shoe removed and the wound dressed as soon as possible, as his foot would swell so that the shoe could not be removed. We could not tell whether those on the stretchers were Confederate or Union soldiers, but I suppose that most of them were Confederates, as they would likely care for their own wounded first.

Julia sings for the troops

That evening, there was a lull as the fighting in the west died down, before the Confederate assault on Greene's Brigade at Culp's Hill got fully underway. After first demanding to be fed, the Rebels in the Front Yard settled for a more sociable request of the Hollinger family – they asked the girls to entertain them with a musical interlude. Even in the midst of a fierce three-day battle, soldiers of any army relish a chance to think of home and hearth, to take a break from dealing with the horror of war. Liberty tells us that

On the evening of Thursday, the second day, a number of Confederates came into the yard and asked father to get them some supper. He said he did not think that we could feed them.

Just then Julia came out of the cellar and stood on the steps which led up into the yard outside the house. The minute they saw her their attitude entirely changed. They became very courteous and politely asked us girls to sing for them. Julia was very patriotic and told them that we would not sing to please Confederates, but that possibly our boys in blue might hear us and be cheered.

So we sang a number of our own Union war songs with which we were familiar. Each time the Confederates would respond with one of their southern songs. Presently an officer rode into the yard and said to one of the men, "Cap, you'd better be careful about these songs." The captain answered, "Why, that's all right. They sing their battle songs, and then we sing ours." They asked us whether we had an instrument, and they wanted to come into the house and have a pleasant social time. But father and mother would not consent.

There was a strong anti-war faction in Gettysburg, led by the Democrat newspaper editor. But the Hollingers were not among them. They might have to tolerate Rebels in their front yard for some entertainment, and they would show them Christian charity, but they were not about to treat the invaders as honored guests.

Chapter 9 July 3: End of the Battle of Gettysburg

Culp's Hill – Southern Assault Repulsed for good

In the late hours of July 2, the battle of Culp's Hill had continued until nearly 11 p.m., when a double bayonet charge by the 137th New York, now out of ammunition, fended off a last charge by attacking Virginians. Reinforcements from regiments of the First Corps had come down from the north slope of the hill, their cartridge cases full, to relieve the exhausted fighters of the 137th, who were then able to move back to resupply their own cartridge cases, clean their muskets, and prepare to renew the fight in the morning.

Slocum's Twelfth Corps was back on the hill in full strength. But Ewell had also committed new Confederate brigades for the planned dawn assault. At 4:30 in the morning, just at first light, the cannonade resumed. Federal guns from across the Baltimore Pike lofted a barrage of shells into the Confederate positions on the lower summit of Culp's Hill. The ground shook for nearly an hour as the cannon balls burst on the hillsides. The Confederate battle lines again moved up the slope, but the Federals of Twelfth Corps, fighting from sturdy breastworks of rock and log, had a huge advantage over the attackers who tried desperately to find cover behind the boulders and trees that broke up their battle lines as they moved up the steep slope. Lee had indeed been right about these hills – it was indeed going to be "difficult to dislodge the troops holding them".

A half-mile north, the Hollinger family had made a brave decision – to remain in their home throughout the calamity that had befallen Gettysburg. They had heeded the advice given them by the young officers of the 134th New York on the first day – go to the cellar and stay there, for safety from the gunfire.

Three Days in the Cellar

We stayed quietly in our cellar most of the time during the three days of the battle. How glad we were for such a safe retreat from all harm and danger! A few bullets struck the cellar doors, and occasionally we could hear them strike the brick walls of the house, but we felt perfectly safe.

We ate cold dinners in the cellar, and sometimes breakfast too. One morning the cannons planted around our house began to shake the house with their unearthly explosions before we were ready to descend. In the evenings, after the firing ceased, we ventured up into the kitchen to cook a hot meal, and we slept upstairs every night.

Such was our life for three days, Wednesday, Thursday and Friday.

Libbie had felt the impact of the dawn bombardment at Culp's Hill on Friday morning, and remembered it. The massive two-hundred cannon two-way bombardment that for two hours preceded, and then accompanied Pickett's Charge on Friday afternoon could only have caused the Hollingers to remain safely in their cellar. The Confederate missiles, mis-aimed or mis-fused, flew over the heads of the Federals on Cemetery Ridge and landed well to the east. The second battle of Culp's Hill ended before noon. Ewell's Confederates retreated back down the slope, leaving behind scores of wounded and dead, with many surrendering. That afternoon, the stray shells from Longstreet's artillery kept the men of the Twelfth Corps annoyed, if not seriously impacted. Presumably none of the errant shells landed anywhere near the York – Hanover Road intersection. In their cellar, while the noise may well have been sufficiently muffled to relieve concern that a shell might hit their house, Libbie and her family prayed that the fighting would soon come to an end. And with the Union Army victorious!

The Battle Ended

With the failure of Ewell's attack on Culp's Hill in the morning, and of Pickett's Charge against the center of the Federal line on Cemetery Ridge on Friday afternoon, the Battle of Gettysburg was effectively at an end. Libbie and Julia Hollinger were grateful that their family had lived safely amid the fighting with minimal damage to home or property. But the horror of battle would remain with them for months, as they dealt with the aftermath of the battle. Saturday, the Confederates remained in the town. The Hollingers would be dealing with yet more encounters with Rebels in the Front Yard.

Chapter 10   July 4: Confederate Retreat

Independence Day in Gettysburg, 1863

Saturday, the Fourth of July, would be quietly celebrated by the Federal Army at Gettysburg. Wounded men had to be gathered in and cared for in makeshift hospitals in barns and tents arrayed around the battlefield to the south of town. In the past three days, more than twenty thousand Union soldiers had been killed or wounded. Caring for their wounded and burying their dead would be a massive task. Thousands of dead horses littered the battlefields. These too would have to be disposed of.

No Celebration in Lee's Army

There was no celebration in Lee's army. They had for the first time suffered a major defeat at the hands of the Army of the Potomac. The Army of Northern Virginia had, like their enemy, suffered more than twenty thousand casualties. Lee had no choice now but to order the preparation for his army to pack up, load the wounded on wagons, and prepare to withdraw back across South Mountain, heading back for some semblance of cover beyond the Potomac in Virginia. His men would bury their dead as best they could in the brief time before the army retreated. The wounded would be taken with them, in a wagon train that stretched out over sixteen miles as it moved westward over the mountain.

But until they finally withdrew, late in the day on Saturday, the weight of the Confederate presence in Gettysburg, alive and dead, would continue to be borne by its citizens. The Confederates of Ewell's Corps that had fought at Cemetery Hill and Culp's Hill had withdrawn late Friday, moving around east and north of the town to gather on the ridge west of the Seminary. A few had remained behind, still tending to the wounded, or commandeering horses and wagons to transport their wounded men away. They had buried some of their comrades, but many more bodies lay where they had fallen.

On Saturday, Libbie and Julia Hollinger continued to deal with Rebel soldiers wanting some last favor before they left town. Some made demands that could not be denied. A few made polite requests that must be honored by a family who practiced true Christian charity for all who asked.

The Hollingers had slept fitfully upstairs in their bedrooms on Friday night, uncertain of what new conflict might erupt on Saturday morning. It would be the Fourth of July, but Jacob Hollinger saw no reason for celebration. Liberty recalled the experience of that Saturday:

On Saturday morning we went downstairs to try to get a little breakfast and soon realized that all was quiet there. We ventured out to look around. The few Confederates seemed to be either wounded or were stragglers. The battle was ended.

General Lee had concluded that renewing the battle that morning would be a futile exercise. His army was exhausted. It was time to withdraw. He gave orders to gather the wounded and load them into wagons for the long trip over the mountain. His men duly searched the town for wagons and horses to pull them. The Hollinger's were not exempted from this confiscation process. Jacob had retired his warehouse draft horse some time ago and brought it home to end his days in comfort at the Hollinger pasture. But this Saturday, even the Hollinger horse would have to bend to the will of the Rebels in their yard. The Confederates were withdrawing and taking the old horse with them, ignoring Jacob's protest that the animal could do them no good.

Rebels take the Hollinger horse

Finally they also took our horse when they retreated on Saturday, but I suppose they soon discovered that father had told them the truth when he said it was too old for service. At any rate they did not take it very far, and a few days later we heard that it was at Hanover. Father went and proved his property and brought it home no worse for the capture and little trip. The animal had been used for many years as a draft horse at the warehouse, and was well known all over the town and through the surrounding country.

All's well that ends well. How the horse wound up 15 miles east at Hanover, when Lee's long line of retreating wagons had headed west, is another one of the small mysteries of the Battle of Gettysburg.

Gettysburg becomes a hospital

The treating of the wounded was a constant struggle for both armies during the three days of fighting, and continued into Saturday. The Union wounded were largely cared for in improvised hospitals set up in the many large barns just south of the battle lines, especially along the Baltimore

Pike and the Taneytown road. The Confederates were being cared for in similar barn-hospitals to the west, near the Chambersburg Pike.

Civilians too were pressed into service to treat the wounded. The public buildings of Gettysburg had been quickly pressed into service by the occupying Confederate army. Churches especially were converted into hospitals, and parishioners felt obligated to assist in the care of the wounded men. Some families even took the wounded into their private homes to care for them.

At Pennsylvania College (now Gettysburg College), the main building was turned into a surgery. Arms and legs irreparably damaged by deadly minie balls left the surgeons no choice but to amputate them. By Saturday morning, a macabre pile of bloody limbs had grown up outside the window of the college building.

Bertie at the carpenter shop surgery

East of the college, on York Street, Jeremiah Culp had his carpenter shop, just four doors toward the square from the Hollingers. When the battle of Kuhn's brickyard was over, the Confederates had commandeered his carpenter shop and turned it into a surgery. There too, a pile of Southern arms and legs had grown up outside the shop window. Alberta Hollinger, "Bertie", just eight years old, walked up York Street on Saturday morning to see what it was that had appeared outside the carpenter's window. She came back and told Julia and Libbie what she saw:

There was an emergency hospital in a carpenter shop not far from our house. The carpenter's bench was used as an operating table, and my sister Bertie, who had gone there several times said that there was a big pile of legs and arms outside the window.

A weary Southern Surgeon on the Porch

As the Confederates began to pack up and get ready to move out, an exhausted surgeon walked out of the sweltering blood-soaked carpenter shop. Standing on York Street, looking east, he saw the Hollinger home with its inviting shady porch. Perhaps these folks would be good enough to allow him to rest there for a bit. Liberty later recalled:

On Saturday afternoon a Confederate surgeon came into the yard, and lifting his hat very politely, asked mother if he might sit on the porch and rest. He was very tall and fine-looking, a perfect gentleman both in appearance and manners. He appeared tired and worn. My sister [Bertie], who was then about nine years old, was standing near him and he took her hand and asked mother if he might hold her on his knee. He said she reminded him so much of his sister's little girl.

Mother and I were busy getting supper, and when it was ready she invited him to eat with us. He declined, very politely, saying that he could not possibly eat anything as he was too weary and heartsick from amputating limbs all day. We could see blood-stains on his boots. No doubt it was in [the carpenter's] *shop that he had been operating. We did not learn his name.*

Jacob tends wounded on battlefield

Jacob Hollinger spent Saturday afternoon on his own mission of mercy, while his family was providing a small measure of solace for the Southern surgeon. He had labored all afternoon in the oppressive heat, carrying water to wounded soldiers North and South, who were made desperate for a drink of cool water by loss of blood, made worse by the maddening heat and humidity. How he wished he could do more for these poor unfortunate victims of this terrible battle.

When Jacob finally came back to his home late in the day, Sarah and Libbie were shocked to see how exhausted he was. They could only hope that a hearty meal and a good night's sleep would revitalize him. For they were sure that next day he would be back out on the battlefield again. Liberty remembered:

There was a great deal of rain after the battle. Some thought that it was because of the heavy cannonading and the explosion of so much ammunition. How we suffered from the awful, awful stench coming from the dead horses and even the dead and wounded soldiers from both armies who were still unburied or uncared for! Father felt that he must help out on the field. Heartsick and soul sick and with aching back he served the terribly wounded with the one thing they clamored for-water, water, until he was ready to drop from exhaustion.

While Jacob was out on the battlefield doing what he could to ease the misery of the wounded men that lay amid the bodies of comrades and foe alike, Sarah, Libbie, Julia and their sisters offered hospitality to soldiers of both North and South. While the Confederate surgeon had politely declined Mrs. Hollinger's invitation to share the family's supper, Union soldiers were only too happy to accept an offer of food.

It was not long before our own Union soldiers began to appear. A number of them came to the house, so tired and hungry that mother invited them in, and began to cut bread for them. She spread the bread with butter and then set out a crock of apple butter, telling them to help themselves. They did so in a hurry and declared that it was "the best stuff they ever ate."

Later in the day father found a number of worn and bedraggled Union soldiers in the barn. We fed them also, and they became very friendly. Among them was a German who fell in love with Julia. He would say to her, "Now, Yulie, you say Chorge no more drink, and Chorge no more drink." He would also repeat the saying that was common among the Germans of the Eleventh Corps. "I fight mit Sigel, but I runs mit Howard."

There were two young soldiers among these who came to visit us a number of times after the war was over. One was a Dr. Agnew, and the other a Mr. Wallace. Many years later, Liberty lived in Gettysburg at the Lutheran Seminary where her husband, Rev. Dr. Jacob Clutz, was a member of the faculty. When veterans returned to the reunions on the battlefield, those that had remembered the kindness of the Hollinger household in the midst of the horror of battle, took time to thank Liberty Augusta for those happier memories.

Chapter 11   July 5: A Sunday like no other

Saturday night would have meant fitful sleep for the Hollingers, despite their tiredness from the day's exertions on behalf of the wounded soldiers. Although the fighting had ended, and the Confederates were headed west over South Mountain, the horrific images of the week would not soon fade from their minds. And they knew that the wreckage of battle, the dead and dying still covered the battlefield and the town. Who would care for the living? Who would bury the dead? Who would compensate the people of Adams County for their losses? It would be a long time before things returned to any kind of normal existence for Liberty Hollinger and her family. Daybreak would surely bring new problems to be faced. Certainly there would be no comforting religious services in Gettysburg that Sunday. Every church was filled with wounded men. Good Christian citizens of Gettysburg would be obligated to help to comfort these soldiers, not seek comfort for themselves.

Liberty later recalled the challenges of that day.

Jacob gathers in the wounded

Sunday, the second day after the battle, and the fifth day of July was a day long to be remembered. It was so different from any other Sunday we had ever known. It had rained very hard Saturday night and the atmosphere was stifling and extremely impure from the many unburied horses and human beings scattered over the vast field. The cavalry field alone covered sixteen square miles and the entire battlefield, forty. On this Sunday morning after the weather had cleared, father, a little rested from the strenuous work of the day before-that terrible Saturday of which I have already written-felt that he must continue to care for the poor wounded and dying men who had fought so bravely. He hitched a horse to the spring wagon, put in plenty of straw to make it as comfortable as possible, and drove out over the battlefield. He brought in many loads of wounded to the emergency hospitals in the churches, the college and seminary.

Neighbors return to ransacked houses

When the Confederates first invaded the town, many residents locked up their houses and fled in fear for their lives. They had abandoned their homes and property, presumably trusting that the Southern soldiers would respect the locked doors. Of course they did not. The invaders broke in and made themselves at home. They helped themselves to whatever they wanted. And when they retreated on Saturday, the Rebels took with them whatever they thought might be useful on the march south. When word reached the residents that the Confederates had departed from Gettysburg, these folks came home. They were shocked at what they found – their houses ransacked, their food gone, the rooms a mess. They bitterly accused those who had remained of failing to protect their abandoned houses. Liberty had little sympathy for their accusations.

Many of our neighbors who had left their homes at the first alarm did not return until everything was quiet. Of course they found their once orderly houses in confusion; beds had been occupied, bureaus ransacked and contents scattered over the house. The larders had been searched for eatables and nothing remained that the soldiers could find use for. We felt indignant, after our terrible experiences to have some of our neighbors blame us because we did not watch over their homes and protect their property. They ignored the ruin and destruction of our own property which we had been powerless to prevent.

They did not seem to realize that to save lives was the sole concern of those frightful days-property and material things faded into the background. We were ready to use ourselves and all we had in service for the men who had saved our town and people. How we studied to serve them in every possible way! We cooked and baked and invited them into our homes and to our tables loaded with all the food we could collect and prepare. Most of our citizens were occupied as we were, helping whenever opportunity offered. True, we had a few people in our town who were dubbed "copperheads" because they did not ring true blue.

Chapter 12   When the Armies Had Gone

The new week saw the citizens of Gettysburg begin to seek a return to normalcy. But of course, the town would never be the same again. To the locals, a great disaster had occurred here, akin to a great flood or a terrible tornado. Though many buildings were undamaged, local farms had been trampled, crops lost, livestock killed, stolen, or lost in the three days of the great battle. The number of dead soldiers of either side, the number of wounded left behind, each far exceeded the population of the town that would have to care for them. In a matter of days, a great influx of visitors, families of the soldiers, spectators, and well-intentioned groups of volunteers would descend upon the town and remain for weeks. The placid pre-invasion routines of the townspeople would be changed forever when Gettysburg became "hallowed ground" as President Lincoln dedicated a new National Cemetery on Cemetery Hill.

Nearly 15,000 Federal soldiers had been wounded, and most were still here. General Lee had gathered up and carried away as many of his wounded Southerners as he could, but many wounded Confederates were left behind for the townspeople and Union surgeons to care for. The churches and public buildings were full of wounded men. Many citizens had taken in wounded men of both armies.

Townswomen & girls minister to the wounded

Liberty Hollinger and her family would join many others, doing their part in trying to clean up the aftermath of battle – tending to both living and dead soldiers left behind by their departing comrades. Their effort helping wounded men in the churches and schools of the town left an indelible record in her mind.

In these buildings and later in the tents put up by the government in the woods east of the town, the women and girls of Gettysburg ministered to the sick and wounded. Many of the temporary nurses laid aside their full hoop-skirts and donned hospital garb so that they might perform their tasks more efficiently.

One day after the Confederates had departed, General Meade assigned his Assistant Adjutant General, Seth Williams, the task of setting up military facilities to care for the wounded. Williams moved swiftly to set up the largest field hospital ever built in North America, Camp Letterman. It was located on the George Wolf farm, just a mile east on the York Pike from the Hollinger home. Dr. Henry James, U. S. Volunteers, took charge of the improvised hospitals scattered throughout the town and surrounding farms, and began to move the wounded to Camp Letterman. This was a huge undertaking – transporting 14,000 Federal and nearly half that number of Confederate soldiers. Those that were able to travel were taken to the railroad depot and sent home or to hospitals in the large cities in the East. Still, more than 4000 remained, in no condition to travel. These were accommodated at Camp Letterman. It was a perfect site – next to the railroad, next to the main road to Philadelphia. It had a natural spring, and a large grove of trees to provide shade in the hot July weather. In many ways, conditions here were more conducive to healing and recovery than the overcrowded metropolitan hospitals. Sarah Hollinger, Libbie and her sisters did everything they could to help, especially by preparing food for the wounded men.

When the hospitals were better established we carried dainties to the wounded and dying of both armies, nearly every day. Mother, especially, was tireless in her willingness to bake and work and to carry cheer and comfort to the suffering soldiers. Of course other women were similarly engaged, both women of Gettysburg and many visitors who came to minister to the wounded.

The Admirable Sisters of Charity from Emmitsburg

The Sisters of Charity from Emmitsburg made their appearance very soon after the battle. I recall many instances of their kindness and usefulness as I watched them sit by the hospital cots, moistening the parched lip, fanning the heated brow, writing a letter to the loved home-folks or reading and praying with the wounded and dying. No wonder the men learned to admire and love them!

Many groups came to Gettysburg to supplement the military nursing staff. The "Patriot Ladies of Lancaster" set out for Gettysburg immediately, and arrived with their supplies just days after the battle. Finding quarters on Chambersburg Street across from Christ Lutheran Church (the college church), they took on the task of cooking food for the wounded crowded into the church, as well as nursing them.

Liberty vividly describes many instances of charity shown to the wounded men:

A kind girl is rewarded with romance with a Southern boy

The young people from the different choirs delighted to sing at the hospitals. Many romances developed. One of our most intimate friends married a southerner whom her mother had nursed back to health. A number of the young ladies were wedded to boys they learned to love while kindly ministering to them.

Mother comforts wounded boys, Blue and Gray

In one of my mother's visits to the hospitals she found a very young Confederate soldier, a mere boy, who was fatally wounded. He seemed so happy to see her, and begged her to come again. He said he loved to look at her because she reminded him of his mother. But, alas! The next time she went to see him she found his cot empty.

Mother also visited a young Union soldier by the name of Ira Sparry who lay badly wounded in the Reformed Church. She was much pleased with his general appearance and manners. He seemed to be getting along all right, and when he learned that his wife was coming to see him he was happy. Their home was in Portland, Maine. She finally arrived and came to our house, but too late to see her husband. He had suddenly taken a turn for the worse, and had died and was buried the day before she reached Gettysburg.

Libbie nurses a wounded Maine boy

This woman (Mrs. Sparry) came to Gettysburg with the father of a wounded boy who was at our house. The boy's right arm had been amputated at the shoulder, and it was my duty to dress the wound every morning and evening. How still he used to hold while I thoroughly cleansed it! His father took him home, and we heard later that though the wound had healed he died from the effects of it. While he was at our house he was so painfully nervous from the pain and shock that he had to have an anodyne [a medicine that was believed to relieve or soothe pain by lessening the sensitivity of the brain or nervous system] *every evening on retiring so as to get some sleep and rest.*

Libbie and Julia at Camp Letterman Army Hospital

Libbie and Julia Hollinger willingly walked the mile east along the York Pike from her home to Letterman Hospital to bring a little companionship and comfort to the wounded patients. Her kindness left an impression with one soldier that stayed with him for a lifetime:

There was a young soldier whom we used to visit in the general hospital which was established in a grove along the York Pike, now the Lincoln Highway. The boy's left foot had been amputated, but he was always very jolly.

The soldier survived the surgery. Sixty years later, he returned to Gettysburg. In those sixty years, Jacob Clutz, the young farm boy on the Taneytown Road, had become the Rev. Dr. Clutz, professor at the Lutheran Seminary. The visiting veteran came to his home on the campus and asked Mrs. Clutz, "had your name been Liberty Hollinger?" At first she didn't recall him, *"but after a little conversation it all came back to me again very clearly."*

Libbie and Julia take a bouquet to Rebel General Trimble

In the weeks after the battle, Liberty and Julia brought comfort and consolation to the wounded in the various other hospitals still remaining in the town. A number of wounded Confederate officers were housed at the Lutheran Seminary, which days before had been in the heart of the Confederate battle line, just down the street from Lee's Headquarters. One of them was General Isaac Trimble, 61. He had come to Gettysburg as an advisor to General Lee. The year before, he had been wounded in the leg at the Second Battle of Bull Run, narrowly avoiding amputation on that occasion. Here at Gettysburg he was again wounded in the leg, while leading Pender's Division during Pickett's Charge. This time the leg was amputated, and he was recovering at the Seminary hospital.

One day Julia and I went out to the Seminary building to see a wounded Confederate officer, Major General Trimble. I do not know how we came to do this, but I remember that we gave him a bouquet of flowers, and that he and his orderly were very polite and kind to us. I little thought then that my husband would be a professor at the seminary and that I would spend so many years on the campus. I think General Trimble made his escape later through the assistance of some southern women who came to Gettysburg after the battle purposely to help Confederate officers to get away.

Though she was right about the southern women facilitating escapes, Liberty was wrong about Trimble. He did not escape. In August he was transferred to a Federal prison at Johnson's Island in Lake Erie, then to Fort Warren in Boston. Trimble had surveyed the Baltimore and Ohio, and had been the Chief Engineer of the Pennsylvania Railroad. His knowledge of the critical points on railroads, both north and south, made him "a dangerous man" to Federal authorities. And with good reason. In the early days of the war, he directed the burning of critical railroad bridges north of Baltimore. It wasn't until March of 1865 when General Ulysses Grant finally authorized his parole. Unrepentant, eager to fight again, he was on his way to re-join Lee's army only to learn of its surrender at Appomattox.

Jacob Hollinger cures soldiers' painful joints

Libbie Hollinger's father possessed unusual folk-healing skills. Nineteenth Century medicine was still rather primitive, and rural families had found ways to cure many ailments without the aid of a physician. One of these ailments they called a "felon", a painful abscess that occurs usually on the end of a finger, thumb, or toe, near the nail. Jacob Hollinger had learned how to cure it, and generously put his skill in practice to aid injured soldiers.

Father acquired a reputation among the soldiers by his ability to cure felons. Many of the men were afflicted in this way and suffered keenly, so that they could not sleep. He would hold the afflicted finger or thumb tightly in his closed hand until the throbbing ceased and the fever left. This was very painful to the sufferers and often tears would pour down their cheeks during the curing process. Father also suffered, feeling the pain sharply in his own hand and arm. But he never failed to effect a cure. The men were so grateful, and they would beg him to let them pay him for the cure, but he would never accept any remuneration from them.

Chapter 13 Visitors Descend on the Town

When the newspapers carried the news of the battle of Gettysburg, people of the North rejoiced. Finally, a great victory for the Union Army! The feared Rebel Invasion had been repulsed. The cities, towns, and farms of the North were safe once more. Then, as the papers published the fearful casualties, many families and friends of the soldiers listed began to make their way to the small town in Pennsylvania. By road and by rail, thousands descended on Gettysburg to search for loved ones, alive or dead.

The first visitors to arrive were shocked at the scenes of death and destruction across the battlefield, scenes that the townspeople had lived with for days. A group of volunteers, The Patriot Ladies of Lancaster, described the scenes of their first encounter with the aftermath of battle:

Houses demolished, fences destroyed, tall forest trees mowed down like so many stalks of hemp; artillery wagons crushed, broken muskets scattered in every direction, unused cartridges in immense numbers, balls of all kinds, ramrods and bayonets, bits of clothing, belts, gloves, knapsacks, letters in great quantities, all lying promiscuously on the field.

Dead horses in great numbers, some torn almost asunder by cannon balls, some pierced in the side by grape shot, and others with their legs completely shot away; some noble chargers apparently kneeling in death, their necks, crested with flowing manes, gracefully arched, as if still proud of the riders on their backs.

And then many of the human dead, whose mutilated bodies, still unburied, were lying around in all positions. Some with their hands gently folded on their breasts, others reclining gracefully on their elbows, and others still leaning against trees, stumps or stones, as if wrapped in the arms of sleep, and given over to sweet dreams.

Like the Lancaster women, many visitors had come to Gettysburg with the best of motives, whether to help the wounded, or to find their soldier in hospital, or sadly, in his grave. Many of the dead would be eventually re-buried in the Gettysburg National Cemetery, but for now, their graves were in the fields where they had fallen in battle. Families had the difficult task of searching out the location of their loved one's body, in order to exhume it and bring it home. The graves of those men whose bodies remained in Gettysburg would be forever in "hallowed ground". Those who had been taken home to a family plot or cemetery would, by their presence, make their final resting place equally hallowed ground.

The Hollinger family did their utmost to assist these travelers, though the terrible stench of decay and death in those first days had made the family quite ill, except for Liberty. To her fell the duty of being the good hostess.

Libbie - hostess for visitors

Among the visitors who came to Gettysburg were friends and acquaintances of our family, many of whom we were glad to welcome. But we could not help being amused, saddened as we were, by some who claimed acquaintance in order to have a stopping-place. As I was the only member of the family who was not suffering from biliousness and illness, I was deputed to receive most of the visitors.

Scavengers on the battlefield

Soon the town began to fill with friends and strangers, some intent on satisfying their curiosity and others, shame to say, to pick up articles of value. Blankets, sabers, guns and many other things were thus obtained and smuggled away or secreted. Some time after the battle when the government began to count up the losses, houses in Gettysburg were searched and some yielded sound and well preserved government property.

Certain of the visitors to Gettysburg had ulterior motives. With some six thousand Confederate soldiers still in hospitals in the town, there were a number of Southern sympathizers who came to Gettysburg intent on assisting in their escape. They knew that as soon as a wounded Confederate soldier was sufficiently recovered, he would be transported off to a Federal prisoner of war camp. These visitors intended to save as many of them as possible from that fate.

A favorite ploy was to provide a wounded soldier, one who was sufficiently recovered and able to travel, with civilian clothes – even women's – to disguise themselves as just other civilian visitors. They would take an outbound train to Baltimore, where sympathizers could readily send them safely on to Confederate territory.

With the huge influx of visitors desperate to find a place to stay, the Hollinger house had become a "bed & breakfast". Accommodating some visitors in their home had unwittingly begun to abet these escape efforts. But when discovered, Jacob Hollinger quickly and forcefully ended it.

Baltimore women come to help Confederates escape

Some southern women came to Gettysburg after the battle purposely to help Confederate officers to get away. Four such ladies from Baltimore were at our house for a few days. They were brought to us and introduced by Dr. John A. Swope who was then living in the town. One was Mrs. Banks and the name of another one was Mrs. Warrington. I do not remember the name of the other two, a lady and her daughter, and am not sure that we ever knew. They were very delightful ladies and were well supplied with money. They spent the whole day out on the field and in the hospitals where the Confederate wounded were.

Their purpose discovered, the Hollingers turn them away

We did not suspect their intentions at first, but when they tried to buy up men's civilian clothes, and even women's clothing, we began to understand what they were about. As soon as my father learned what their real mission was, he insisted that mother must send them away. He would not tolerate any Confederate sympathizers in our house. He had seen too much of what our brave men had suffered because of the war, especially in the Battle of Gettysburg.

The ladies begged very earnestly to be allowed to stay, saying that they were much pleased with their accommodations. They especially liked mother's tea and hot biscuits, and in fact everything she put on the table. Mother was sorry to send them away as they were willing to pay well for every attention. They even offered to increase the amount, but father was relentless. He was not willing to sacrifice his principles, even though the losses he had suffered during the war made ready money very desirable. The four ladies left our home very reluctantly and we could not help wondering whether they found another place they liked.

Dr. Mary Walker

Among the more noble visitors to Gettysburg was a rare curiosity for the mid-nineteenth century – a female physician. Dr. Mary Walker was then 31 years old. A native of Oswego, New York, she had graduated from Syracuse Medical College. When the Civil War began, she asked to serve as a medical officer in the Union Army. They would take her only as an unpaid volunteer. She worked as an unpaid field surgeon near the front lines, which had brought her to Gettysburg in July. But two months later, she would prove her worth at the Battle of Chickamauga, the Army of the Cumberland would award her a commission, and so she would become the first-ever female U.S. Army surgeon.

One of the familiar figures on the streets in those days that interested us very much was Dr. Mary Walker. Her low silk hat, with bloomers, and a man's coat and collar, seemed invariably to call forth a laugh or a yell from the young boys, and many a smile and shrug from the older people.

Chapter 14 Hallowed Ground

July 5 – Union Soldiers bury their dead

On Sunday morning, July 5, their enemy having departed, Federal soldiers finished the sad task of gathering the bodies of dead comrades and burying them in burying grounds hastily laid out in farm fields near where they had fought and died. One such site was on the Spangler farm, below Culp's Hill by the Baltimore Pike. There, among the seventy federal dead were twenty five from the 137th New York, a regiment who had fought so valiantly to hold Culp's Hill on the night of July 2, and helped repulse the final Confederate assault the next morning.

The survivors of the 137th had begun burying their comrades as soon as the fighting ended. Private Sam Lusk wrote: "the firing ceased on the fourth and we buried the dead. We buried the dead of the brigade in one burying ground. They were about two feet apart. We were a hard looking set of fellows when the battle was over, our faces black as coal, our clothes covered with blood and dirt." Private Henry Bayless added: "We lost many a poor boy in our regiment. The fourth we buried our dead; it was a painful duty." On July 5, the Confederates were gone, leaving their dead behind for the Federals to deal with. Private Oscar Severson wrote: "this morning I went over the field where the Rebs fought. The dead lay all over the ground. Our men are burying both our dead and the rebs."

Dead on the Battlefield at Gettysburg

Courtesy of Library of Congress,

Prints & Photographs Division, LC-B171-0256 DLC

The battlefield where Coster's Brigade had fought the Confederates under Hayes and Avery was only two blocks from the Hollinger home. By July 5, Hays and Avery had retreated, Coster having come down off Cemetery Hill in pursuit. On Sunday morning the Federal burial squads went to work. They gathered sixty bodies from the Kuhn brickyard and laid them in rows just south of Stevens Run. They dug graves and interred them there.

Liberty, Julia, and Annie had but a short walk past their father's warehouse on Stratton Street to see first-hand the terrible aftermath of armies in mortal combat. By the time the girls walked over the fields near Kuhn's Brickyard, the bodies had been buried, Coster's men in their fresh graves by

Stevens Run. The Confederate dead were given less attention, doubtless, and lay under just a thin layer of soil, soon to be thinned ever further by the hard rains of the following days. Liberty describes the sights that greeted them:

Gruesome sights on the battlefield

Being occupied in this way [seeing to their house guests] *and in caring for the other members of the family, I did not get out on the battlefield for some time, but when I did find time to go, there was still much to horrify. Many trenches in which soldiers were buried were necessarily very shallow and gruesome sights greeted those who came near. It was not unusual to see a hand or foot or other part of the body protruding from the ground. To conceal skeletons from view, I would collect army coats lying about and place them over the bones.*

Annie finds a hand on the battlefield

When my sister Annie was walking over the field, several weeks after the battle, she picked up a hand, dried to parchment so that it looked as though covered with a kid glove. There was nothing repulsive about the relic, and we all remarked about the smallness of the fingers. We guessed that it must have belonged to a very young soldier or a southerner who had never worked with his hands.

1854 – Gettysburg builds a cemetery – Ever Green

In the Nineteenth Century, death was never far from any family, even before the terrible toll of Civil War. Children died young, mothers died in childbirth, men died early from disease and accidents. For the most part, farm families had a small plot, often in a grove of trees, where their dead were laid, close to where the family could mourn them. Or they were laid to rest in a nearby country churchyard. In the 1830's, towns began to build "cemeteries", where the townspeople could lay their dead to rest, and where they could come to mourn, to commune with family members and friends who had gone on before them.

In 1854, Gettysburg citizens led by David McConaughy established a fine new cemetery on a hill at the south edge of town. They gave it the name Ever Green (in later years the words were combined to "Evergreen", as it is known today). Designed by a prominent Philadelphia architect, Ever Green became a fine example of the newly fashionable "garden cemetery". At its entrance off the Baltimore Pike, sat the imposing brick Gate House, which also served as residence for the caretakers, Peter Thorn and his wife Elizabeth on one side, her parents on the other. Little did the Thorn family realize the death and destruction that would be centered there on Cemetery Hill, a mere eight years after the Gate House was erected. Or that 3500 fallen soldiers would then be buried in a new cemetery abutting Ever Green.

Evergreen Cemetery, Gettysburg Battlefield

Photo by the author

Soon after the battle, the town fathers of Gettysburg realized that a more permanent repository was needed for the Union's heroic dead. A fitting burial ground, at least as handsome as the town's own, was needed. America was deeply impressed by the new vogue of the "garden cemetery". Proponents believed that burying and commemorating the dead was best done in a tranquil and beautiful natural setting just a short distance from the town center. The "Cemetery" should be a place for the living, park-like – with monuments, fences, fountains and chapels set in a natural landscape enhanced by ornamental plants shrubs and trees.

Hallowed Ground - Gettysburg National Cemetery

With the successful creation of Ever Green Cemetery fresh in his mind, McConaughy proposed that an addition to it be made, in which to re-inter the North's fallen heroes. With the active support of Pennsylvania Governor Curtin, a group of prominent citizens, led by Judge David Wills, purchased a tract of land south of the village, on the north boundary of Ever Green Cemetery. Governor Curtin made state funds available to hire laborers to for the difficult task of exhuming bodies from their hastily dug graves and moving the remains to new graves in what would be called the Gettysburg National Cemetery. Designed by architect William Saunders,

the graves were laid out in semi-circles, centered on the Soldiers National Monument, which was erected at the top of the hill, adjacent to the town cemetery.

Over the next 4 months, bodies were disinterred and removed to the new cemetery. Wanting to dedicate the cemetery before winter snows covered the ground, Wills and his friends arranged for a dedication ceremony to be held on Nov 19. They invited the greatest orator of his time, Edward Everett Horton, to deliver the dedicatory speech. As a courtesy, they also invited President Lincoln to attend, and make a few remarks.

The Hollinger family followed the progress of the new cemetery development with great interest, and naturally were excited, as were all the citizens of Gettysburg, to learn that among the many dignitaries coming for the dedication would be the President himself. They knew there were those (many, even) in Gettysburg who held Lincoln responsible for the War, and hence for the terrible calamity that had befallen them in July. But he was, a celebrity, and the President of the United States – and he was coming to their town. Of course, there were many like the Hollingers who were strong supporters of the Union, and of their beloved President Lincoln.

Chapter 15 November 1863: Liberty and Lincoln

"Let's go over to McCreary's!"

On the 19th of November, 1863, Gettysburg was full of strangers. Everywhere there was excitement. Of a different nature, of course, but nearly as much as there was when the battle was fought. Liberty Hollinger had just turned 17. Libby, sister Julia, and their friends were eager to go downtown to the "Diamond" (Gettysburg's town square) and try to catch a glimpse of the President. They had heard that he was staying at the home of Judge David Wills, on Baltimore Street at the Diamond.

Judge David Wills house, 1889

Courtesy of Wills House Museum

Mr. McCreary owned a handsome home just across Baltimore Street from Judge Wills. The girls knew the McCreary's – knew they'd be welcome there. Excited, one of them said "Let's go over to McCreary's!" The kind McCreary family opened the door to the girls and led them to an upstairs room that had large windows overlooking Baltimore Street. Indeed, they had a view directly into the upper rooms of the Wills house.

The President and some members of his cabinet, and also our own beloved Governor Curtin of Pennsylvania, were entertained at the home of Judge Wills, one of the town's most prominent and patriotic citizens of the day, and the man who originated the idea of gathering the dead soldiers for interment in one place, and also the idea of preserving the battlefield itself as nearly as possible as it was left after the battle.

We could see everything distinctly. On the front steps, Governor Curtin and some of the others were greeting people as they passed, shaking hands, laughing, joking, slapping Bill and Joe on the back, having a jolly good time generally. Once in a while a group of pretty girls would pass by. Governor Curtin, who seemed to be the prince of good fellows, kissed every one who gave him the opportunity. And then there was more laughter, the teasing, and joking.

Liberty sees Lincoln

"There's the President!" Julia suddenly cried out. "Where?" Everyone wanted to know as they crowded closer to the windows. He certainly wasn't among the laughing, jolly crowd on Judge Wills' front steps.

"There! Don't you see him? In that front room over there upstairs on the second floor!" We could distinctly see him pacing back and forth, in his room, just before the forming of the procession to the cemetery, apparently engaged in deep thought. I suppose he was preparing for his address. Twice he came to the window and looked out on the street, and each time he held in his left hand a piece of yellow paper about the size and appearance of an ordinary envelope such as was in common use at that time.

A hush stole over our little group of girls as we watched the President of our country. My chief impression was of the inexpressible sadness of his face, which was in so marked contrast with what was going on down below where all was excitement and where everyone was having such a jolly time.

"How can they?" Perhaps he was thinking. "How can they be so light-hearted and frivolous when right now we are engaged in a great Civil War, testing whether our nation or any nation so conceived and so dedicated can long endure. We are about to meet on a great battlefield of that war, and to dedicate a portion of it as a final resting *place for those who here gave their lives that our nation might live? How can they be so carefree and gay?" And yet he would have been the last person on earth to chide them for their light-hearted laughter.*

Poor Mr. President! Abraham Lincoln had to bear the brunt of the Civil War on his shoulders; he was accused openly and secretly of having been the direct cause of the war, and even some members of his own party quibbled and engaged with petty fault-finding with the way he was conducting the war. He knew there were people right here in Gettysburg who believed it was his fault the battle of Gettysburg had to be fought and so many lives lost, lives of their husbands, sons, and brothers. Is it any wonder the face of Abraham Lincoln was inexpressibly sad?

Lincoln's horse "pranced around quite lively"

Lincoln (in top hat) on horseback amid the crowd at Gettysburg

(Detail of photograph by Alexander Gardner), *Library of Congress*

By and by it was time for the procession to be formed, and President Lincoln came down to take the place in line. I well remember the appearance of Mr. Lincoln with his high silk hat. They gave him a rather small horse, and when he mounted it his feet almost touched the ground.

Mr. Lincoln did not come down until most of the crowd had left for the cemetery. It is about half a mile from the center of town where Mr. Lincoln was entertained, and in their eagerness to get good places to see and hear, those who would not take part in the procession hastened out in advance. About a hundred students from the Lutheran College located here [now Gettysburg College] were gathered in the street just opposite the Wills residence waiting to take their place in the procession. I assure you they all cheered most heartily when the President appeared.

Governor Curtin was the Master of Ceremonies, and rode by the side of the President in the procession. As the procession started, the band began to play and Mr. Lincoln's horse became excited and pranced around quite lively. It seemed to amuse the President, and then that sober, sad-faced man actually smiled.

There were also many cavalrymen present to act as a guard of honor for the President, and of course they cheered and saluted, so there did not seem to be any lack of demonstration and enthusiasm. We certainly saw no sign of hostility or unfriendliness. The President seemed to be pleased with these greetings and answered by bows and smiles, bows and smiles, as he rode along. For the time it seemed like sunshine on his face.

The students who were waiting to join the procession were greatly disappointed when they found themselves held back and placed at the tail end of the procession. But when they reached the cemetery, the troops acting as guard of honor were halted, and the students were allowed to pass on with the President and other visitors, and thus got a place right in front of the speakers' stand to their great delight.

Your brief address will endure long after mine is forgotten.

Because of the great crowd my sister and I and the girl friends we were with, did not go to the cemetery. Hence I did not hear the addresses there. But I remember that [College President] Baugher heard Mr. Everett, who had delivered the chief oration, congratulate the President, and say to him "Your brief address will endure long after mine, which was over an hour in delivery, will be forgotten". The great orator recognized the jewels in President Lincoln's address, the most wonderful ever spoken in the English language.

For many years it was assumed that Lincoln made his remarks on the grounds of the National Cemetery. But more recent analysis of photographs indicates that the speakers' platform was actually erected on the grounds of Evergreen Cemetery. Had she stood there on November 1863, Libbie would have heard those immortal words direct from Lincoln's own lips:

"Four score and seven years ago our fathers brought forth on this continent, a new nation, conceived in Liberty, and dedicated to the proposition that all men are created equal.

Now we are engaged in a great civil war, testing whether that nation, or any nation so conceived and so dedicated, can long endure. We are met on a great battle-field of that war. We have come to dedicate a portion of that field, as a final resting place for those who here gave their lives that nation might live. It is altogether fitting and proper that we should do this.

But, in a larger sense, we can not dedicate -- we can not consecrate -- we can not hallow -- this ground. The brave men, living and dead, who struggled here, have consecrated it, far above our poor power to add or detract. The world will little note, nor long remember what we say here, but it can never forget what they did here. It is for us the living, rather, to be dedicated here to the unfinished work which they who fought here have thus far so nobly advanced. It is rather for us to be here dedicated to the great task remaining before us -- that from these honored dead we take increased devotion to that cause for which they gave the last full measure of devotion -- that we here highly resolve that these dead shall not have died in vain -- that this nation, under God, shall have a new birth of freedom -- and that government of the people, by the people, for the people, shall not perish from the earth."

So it seems poetic justice that Liberty Hollinger now rests for eternity in Evergreen Cemetery, just down the hill from the place where Lincoln spoke those 272 memorable words.

Monument, Jacob A.Clutz, D. D. and wife Liberty A. Hollinger

Photo by author

Chapter 16 July 1913: Gettysburg's 50th Reunion

Fifty years passed. In 1913, Liberty Hollinger was living in a large brick home on the campus of the Lutheran Seminary at Gettysburg where her husband, the Reverend Dr. Jacob A. Clutz, was Professor of Practical Theology.

Liberty and a dashing young cavalryman

The Hollinger family had known Jacob since he was lad of 15, attending the Preparatory School (later called Gettysburg Academy) affiliated with Pennsylvania College. Christ Lutheran Church on Chambersburg Street was "the college church", and Jacob began attending there in the fall of 1863 when he entered the Academy. He and the Hollinger girls, Libbie and Julia, would have become acquainted, as their family had long been members of Christ Lutheran. The next summer, 1864, Jacob "inspired with patriotic spirit", enlisted in the Union Army at the age of 16, and served as a member of Warren's Rangers, Mounted Infantry, from July to November. As a dashing young cavalryman, Jacob doubtless impressed the Hollinger girls when he attended church in his uniform. As the Civil War ended in 1865, Jacob continued his education, graduating from Gettysburg College in 1869, and immediately entered the Lutheran Seminary. All during this time, with his regular Sunday attendance at Christ Lutheran Church, Jacob became ever more attracted to Libbie Hollinger, and she to him.

Following his graduation from the Seminary at Gettysburg, a newly-ordained Lutheran minister, he asked Jacob Hollinger for his eldest daughter's hand in marriage. With an appointment in hand as the pastor of the Lutheran Church in Newville PA, the new minister was financially able to support a wife. Jacob Hollinger gladly gave him his blessing.

A wedding at "Roselawn"

Jacob Hollinger had done well enough in the lumber and grain business in the years after the battle to move to a lovely home "in the suburbs". "Roselawn" was located on Table Rock Road just a mile and a half north of their war-time home in Gettysburg. On September 4, 1872, family and friends gathered at "Roselawn" to celebrate the marriage of Liberty Augusta Hollinger to the Rev. Jacob Abraham Clutz. Libbie was now 25, Jacob 24.

Liberty Augusta Hollinger & Jacob Abraham Clutz, 1872

(collection of Henry Clutz)

The new couple moved west over South Mountain to Newville, where soon their child, Frank Hollinger Clutz, was born, on June 29, 1873, just ten years after the Confederate army approached Gettysburg, to begin what would become known as the Battle of Gettysburg. After two years as a small-town pastor, Jacob was called to the pastorate of St. Paul's Church in Baltimore. Liberty and her family would live there for the next ten years. In 1889, a new Lutheran college was founded in Atchison, Kansas. The Rev. Jacob Clutz was named as President, Midland College.

Remembering Gettysburg in Kansas

While in Kansas, some thirty years after she witnessed the Battle of Gettysburg, Liberty found herself recalling the events of her teen years, as she recounts here:

Many years after the Battle of Gettysburg, when we had moved to Kansas, we were sometimes reminded of the events of those bygone days. Mr. Hursh, the father of one of the students at Midland College, of which my husband was president, invited us to visit his home in Lancaster, Kansas. He had been in Gettysburg after the battle, serving in the Quartermaster's Department. He told us of various people he had met and mentioned among others a "fine gray-haired gentleman who had a grain and lumber yard." He said he never saw anyone so devoted to Bible reading. Much pleased, I told him who the man was-my father.

After 15 years in Kansas, Liberty and Jacob moved their family back to their home town. The Reverend Dr. Clutz had accepted a call to the pastorate of St. James Church, where he served for five years. In 1910, he became Professor of Practical Theology at the Lutheran Seminary. He and Liberty moved into a large brick home on the campus that had been built there before the Civil War.

Blue and Gray reconciled at last

With the fiftieth anniversary of the Battle of Gettysburg, July 1-3, 1913, veterans of both armies descended on the town. Liberty described the reunion of these old comrades and opponents.

What an eventful ten days they were when the Blue and the Gray – old veterans were provided with transportation, distance and expense not considered. What beautiful, brotherly fellowship was everywhere in evidence among them, where once was bitterness and hatred. How the manifest appreciation of our great government was expressed in every way towards the old soldier, softening all resentment that once existed. Surprising scenes of real kindness were often observed by others, and many interesting stories were related after the anniversary by the witnesses of such occurrences.

The veterans realized they were being royally entertained. Everything that could be done for their comfort and convenience was in evidence. Mr. Clutz had a standing invitation to be one of them. Since he was in his own home in the town, he did not accept fully, but sometimes mingled with the boys and ate the food provided with much relish.

President Wilson at Gettysburg, 1913 *(Library of Congress)*

I remember we all went with him on New York Day. That was the day the President [Woodrow Wilson] *was to be here to make his speech to the old and thinning ranks. He came out to the camp in a private railroad car, hastily mounted the platform, and after a short address to the many veterans before him, left the grounds just as hastily as he came, speaking to but very few. I could not help feeling that great disappointment was evident among the old soldiers, whose patriotism had seemingly been forgotten or lightly cherished by the head of our government.*

The Blue and Gray at Gettysburg, 1913 *(Library of Congress)*

We felt well repaid for our time and effort in going out to the field to hear and see, heard many speeches from representative men both from the North and South. What a real treat it was to look into their happy faces and hear their cheery words and realize that all unkind feelings and bitterness of strife had been forever banished from mind and heart. Gettysburg was a very, busy, bustling town with great crowds of visitors. Many of the homes were full. Surely it was a great time, never to be forgotten.

Liberty Augusta Hollinger saw first-hand the terrible fury unleashed by American men on one another at Gettysburg in the summer of 1863. It was to some, the War of Southern Independence, or the War Between the States. To others, it was the War of the Rebellion. Later, it was generally referred to as The American Civil War.

In 1913, Liberty Hollinger Clutz witnessed the healing that time brings, even to the most terrible deadly enmity. There on the battlefield where their comrades had died or suffered wounds that shortened lives, these Americans now gathered and shook hands. They had faced death in battle, suffered hardship and privation, and were still alive to tell the tale. Others may still harbor the resentments or hatred that led to the war. But not these veterans. As they stood by the monuments that honored their deeds of valor, they felt the bond of shared experience at Gettysburg. It was enough to erase the stains of hatred and contempt that had driven them to heroic heights on that battlefield, fifty years before.

Sixty years after the Battle of Gettysburg

Liberty never lost the images formed at age sixteen. The Battle of Gettysburg, the greatest battle ever fought in North America, had firmly set those experiences in her mind. She tells the reader:

The time I have spent in recalling to mind and writing out these memories of the Battle of Gettysburg has been of mingled pleasure and pain. Living over the days when our family was an unbroken circle has brought back the joy of childhood and youth; but I cannot help feeling again some of the mental and physical strain under which we passed our days and nights. This very tenseness served to fix impressions in my young mind so indelibly that now when I have grown old, I find them clear and undimmed.

End Notes

The Liberty Hollinger Memoir:

In 1926, the newly-widowed Liberty Augusta Hollinger Clutz was living at the home of her daughter. The previous September Rev. Dr. Jacob Clutz, Professor of Theology and Homiletics at the Gettysburg Lutheran Theological Seminary, went abroad to a Lutheran Conference in Stockholm, Sweden. He was accompanied by their son, Frank Hollinger Clutz. There Jacob suffered a tragic death, reported in *Alumni Records of Gettysburg College, 1832-1932*: *He died, suddenly, of heart failure on a train after he had proceeded one hour from Stockholm, Sweden, where he had attended the Universal Conference on Life & Work. When the Conference was about half over, in crossing a street, Dr. Clutz was struck by a motor truck, hurled to the curb, and seriously injured about the head. To the surprise of the physicians at the hospital, he rallied sufficiently to be allowed to start on his homeward journey after ten days. But he had scarcely taken the train before he collapsed.* One can only imagine the sadness that his son Frank would have endured on the long ocean voyage back to New York, knowing the impact the loss would have had on his mother, waiting in Gettysburg.

With his death, their long-time home on the Seminary Campus reverted back to the school. Liberty moved to the home of her daughter, Ruth (Mrs. Mark Eckert). The Eckerts lived just a block further down the hill on Springs Avenue. So while she had lost her husband of 53 years, many friends from their life at the Seminary still lived close by.

One of these was Mrs. Lewars – the author Elsie Singmaster. She also lived on campus, just across Seminary Avenue. Her father, the Rev. Dr. John Singmaster, had been a member of the Seminary faculty for many years. Elsie, too, was a widow. While living in Harrisburg, her husband of three years, Harold Lewars, died after an illness. Two months later her newborn son also died. Mrs. Lewars moved back to Gettysburg, and perhaps to assuage her grief, immersed herself in the prolific writing career she had begun in 1905. As "Elsie Singmaster", she wrote many short stories and articles for, among others, the Atlantic Monthly. Over a 40 year career, she authored 42 books, both novels and Pennsylvania histories. Elsie had long known Liberty, and had become close friends with Ruth Eckert, and with Sarah Baker Clutz, Liberty's daughter-in-law, whose husband Dr. Frank Clutz was on the faculty of Gettysburg College. They met weekly as a social group that they christened "Tea Cups".

Liberty had been a close partner of her husband, from his first assignment as a Lutheran pastor in the small town of Newville, to his Presidency of Midland College in Kansas, and to his return to their native Adams County at the Seminary. At seventy-eight, she was still active and vital. Ruth and Sara decided she needed a stimulating project to utilize her energy and talent and to relieve her grief. They knew just the project, and just the person to encourage and assist Liberty in bringing it to fruition – their friend Elsie Singmaster. She could persuade Liberty to write the memoir that recounted the experience of the Battle of Gettysburg, just as Liberty had lived it. Over tea, Elsie Singmaster was enlisted in their cause.

Elsie Singmaster later wrote these words about Liberty Hollinger Clutz and her memoir:

LIBERTY AUGUSTA HOLLINGER was sixteen years old at the time of the Battle of Gettysburg, the eldest of a family of four girls and one boy, living with their parents at the eastern end of the pleasant, tree-shaded town.

Mrs. Clutz speaks with naive admiration of the beauty of her young sister. She herself retained until her death at the age of eighty-one the characteristic charm of her family. In Gettysburg, her large family married and gone, Mrs. Clutz was happy in her garden, her friends and her books. She never ceased to believe that the Civil War was a sad necessity; she always revered Abraham Lincoln.

In attendance at a religious convocation in Sweden, Dr. Clutz was struck by a car and fatally injured. With the same fortitude with which she had ministered to the wounded in her girlhood, Mrs. Clutz endured this overwhelming shock during the few years of life which remained.

Her reminiscences were written in 1925, sixty-two years after the battle. They are remarkable only as any simple, vivid narrative is remarkable. They are especially interesting because they show the calmness and efficiency with which the citizens of Gettysburg, even children, met the most terrible of disasters.

In 1925, Mrs. Clutz had this memoir printed:

SOME PERSONAL RECOLLECTIONS OF THE

BATTLE OF GETTYSBURG,

BY MRS. JACOB A. CLUTZ

(Liberty Augusta Hollinger)

The memoir began with these words:

My children, and other members of our family, have often expressed a wish that I would make some permanent record of my recollections of the Battle of Gettysburg. So many years have passed that many things have entirely escaped my memory. But this year, 1925, the anniversary of the battle has happened to fall again on Wednesday, Thursday and Friday. Somehow this fact has served to recall the more vividly the scenes and horrors of those three days of bloody fighting between the two great armies. In imagination I live it all over almost as though it were just occurring. So many vivid pictures crowd my mind and fill my soul, that I almost fear to try to describe them as they occurred. But I will do the best I can.

There were just fifty copies printed. The author's family has copy number 41, inscribed in her handwriting:

To a little pupil

Miss Annie Major

(signed) *Mrs. Liberty Augusta Clutz*

The copy she gave to her son, Frank Hollinger Clutz, then a professor of Engineering at Gettysburg College, is now in the collection of the Adams County Historical Society, on the campus of the Lutheran Theological Seminary. Given her long tenure as a resident on the Seminary campus, there is no more appropriate institution for her Memoir to be preserved.

The author hopes that this book, *Rebels in the Front Yard,* has made her invaluable descriptions more readily accessible to the general public, especially those who seek more understanding of the role of Gettysburg's citizens during that great battle at Gettysburg.

The Maria Shultz Memoir

Maria's memoir was found by the author in the collection of Catherine Hartman Clutz. Catherine's mother Elizabeth Forney Hartman and Maria shared a Forney great-grandfather in Hanover. In 1920, Mrs. Hartman and Maria Shultz lived near each other on the west end of Gettysburg. In her own memoir, Catherine Clutz gives this account of a visit to Maria Shultz:

Lilies of the Valley always remind me of the field of wild ones which grew around the little old house where cousin Maria Shultz lived on Confederate Ave. It was only a short walk from our house on Springs Ave. and frequently Mother would take me to visit Maria, for the sole purpose of checking on her aged distant cousin, who lived alone. I remember a thin little old lady, bent and wrinkled – wearing a sunbonnet always, to protect her failing eyes – gladly, almost grabbing the basket from Mother's hand, which she was anxious to explore, would find the goodies which Mother had prepared for her. While she placed the fresh vegetables and butter and fruit and dishes on her well scrubbed kitchen table, I was told to go and help myself to all the lilies of the valley I could pick in the short time we were there. I loved the spot.

Maria's mother was Elizabeth Forney, a sister of mother's grandfather, Karle. She was married to David Shultz, once a lawyer of Hanover, Pa. She was a woman of great spirit and strong family pride. During the latter part of her life she lived in Gettysburg in a large brick house on Seminary Ridge (Confederate Ave.), the scene of the first day's battle in 1863. Her daughter, Maria, was the last of her family when I knew her, but she recorded what it was like to be living, a young woman, in the midst of battle.

Eternal Connections of Liberty Hollinger and Samuel Forney

Liberty Hollinger began life as a child in Gettysburg, married a Gettysburg boy, the Rev. Dr. Jacob A. Clutz, and spent her late life in Gettysburg. In between, she lived in a small town in Pennsylvania and in the city of Baltimore as the wife of a Lutheran pastor. She accompanied him to Kansas, when he became the first President of Midland College. When he later returned to Gettysburg to the faculty of the Lutheran Seminary, Liberty and Jacob took up residence in the imposing home on Seminary Ridge. Following Jacob's untimely death, Liberty moved in with her daughter Ruth Eckert, just a block down the hill on Springs Avenue. There, with the encouragement of Ruth and her friends, and her son Frank and his wife Sara Baker Clutz, she wrote her "Recollections of the Battle of Gettysburg". Liberty likely knew her neighbor, Maria Shultz, then living nearby on Confederate Avenue. Perhaps Maria's account of the battle helped inspire Liberty to write her own. When Liberty passed away, she was buried next to Jacob in Evergreen Cemetery, on the Battlefield, just a short distance down the hill from the site of Lincoln's Gettysburg Address.

Samuel Forney, as the eldest son of Karle Forney, was heir to the Hanover farm on which so much of the Battle of Hanover had occurred. He remained there, and married Mary Catherine Young. They had three daughters, Minnie (later Mrs. John Fleming), Laura (Mrs. Mackelduff), and Elizabeth (Mrs. Harry Hartman). In the twentieth century, the Forney farm would be developed for housing in southwest Hanover. Street names there carry the family names (Forney, Fleming, Hartman) alongside those of the cavalrymen who had fought on that ground (Stuart, Kilpatrick).

Liberty's grave is just a short distance north of the grave of her daughter, Ruth Eckert. Across the road to the south is the Clutz family plot with the graves of her son Frank and his wife Sara, their sons John and Dr. Paul, and Paul's wife Catherine. A few yards closer is the plot of

Catherine's parents, Dr. Harry Hartman and wife Elizabeth, daughter of Samuel Forney. In due time the author will be buried in his family plot adjacent to his parents and grandparents - the blood tie, with his brothers, of the Hollinger and Forney families. Here then is an eternal connection to Gettysburg and Hanover, the Battle of Gettysburg, and indeed to the earliest days of York and Adams County, Pennsylvania.

Descendants of Liberty Augusta Hollinger Clutz (partial list)

1. Frank Hollinger Clutz*	1a Sara Baker Clutz*
1.2a Mary Catherine Hartman Clutz (Mrs. Paul A.Clutz*)	1.2.1 Henry Alexander Clutz
1.2.2 William Hartman Clutz*	1.2.3 David Archibald Clutz*
2. Ruth Augusta Clutz Eckert*	2a Mark Kurtz Eckert*
2.1 Mark Anthony Eckert*	2.1a Mary Alice Eckert*
2.2 Richard Hollinger Eckert	
3. Julia Troxell Clutz Peters	3a Robert John Peters
4.1 Frank Hiatt Clutz	

*Evergreen Cemetery, Gettysburg

Photo taken ca 1939, Gettysburg

Sources:

Chapters One and Two:

Mary Catherine Hartman Clutz – *A Family Memoir*, privately printed, June, 1993

Hanover Chamber of Commerce: *Prelude to Gettysburg – Encounter at Hanover,* Burd Street Press, 1962

Private papers of the Forney/Hartman families, collection of Jennifer Olexy Herring

History of York County, John Gibson, 1886

War Years with Jeb Stuart, Lt. Col. W. W. Blackford, C.S.A., Louisiana State University Press, 1993

Chapter Three:

Mary Catherine Hartman Clutz – *A Family Memoir*, privately printed, June, 1993

Samuel P. Bates, *History of Pennsylvania volunteers, 1861-5*; prepared in compliance with acts of the legislature,

Steven W. Sears, *Chancellorsville*, Houghton Mifflin, New York, 1996

Chapters Three through Sixteen:

Some Personal Recollections of the Battle of Gettysburg, Mrs. Jacob A. Clutz (Liberty Augusta Hollinger), private printing, 1926

Gettysburg – A Testing of Courage, Noah Andre Trudeau, Harper Collins, 2002

Chapter Five:

The Descendants of Johann Jacob Klotz in North America, R. D. Kluttz, Salisbury, NC, 1990

Chapter Six:

Report of the Adjutant General of the State of New York, page 652, 134th New York Volunteers, Albany, 1904

The Coster Avenue Mural in Gettysburg, Mark H. Dunkelman, Providence, 1989

Chapters Eight and Fourteen:

Fields of Fame & Glory: Col. David Ireland and the 137th New York, A Regimental History David Cleutz, XLibris, 2010

Chapter Fourteen:

Hospital Scenes After the Battle of Gettysburg, By the Patriot Daughters of Lancaster, 1864

Chapter Sixteen

Beyond the Gatehouse – Gettysburg's Evergreen Cemetery Brian A. Kennell, Sheridan Press, Hanover, 2000

Acknowledgements

The author gratefully acknowledges the assistance of many who contributed to his research. In Gettysburg, Wayne Motts and his volunteers at the Adams County Historical Society; Lisa Malandra Shower and Tim Smith for details of the citizens of York Street: Bernadette Loeffel-Atkins for pointing me to the Mark Dunkelman booklet on the Coster Avenue Mural. At Gettysburg College, Karen Drickamer and Carolyn Sautter for their assistance. In Hanover, Fletcher Hiigel of the Guthrie Memorial Library; Fred Clark for his effort in photographing the Becker paintings in the Guthrie Library.

Sandy Hartman Olexy and Jennifer Herring gave me access to Forney family photos and information. Henry Clutz had carefully preserved many photos and records of Liberty Hollinger and Jacob Clutz. William Clutz shared family data from Gettysburg.

Thanks are due to the following for their encouragement and support in the writing of the book. Bernadette Loeffel-Atkins inspired me to write a book that gave insight into the stories of Gettysburg civilians during the Battle. My wife Terry encouraged the writing and research, and proof-read and suggested improvements to the early drafts. Catherine Daniell helped to edit early drafts. To others who I may have failed to recognize for your help and encouragement, I beg your pardon.

Finally, thanks to the independent bookstores that make books like this available to interested readers, and thus serve to preserve and enhance wider understanding of Civil War history.

CPSIA information can be obtained
at www.ICGtesting.com
Printed in the USA
BVHW010557130919
558379BV00005BB/105/P